Beauty from Ashes

Readings for times of loss

Published by
The Bible Reading Fellowship
15 The Chambers, Vineyard
Abingdon OX14 3FE
United Kingdom
Tel: +44 (0)1865 319700; Email: enquiries@brf.org.uk
Website: www.brf.org.uk
BRF is a Registered Charity

ISBN 978 1 84101 744 0

First published 2000 (Reprinted five times)
This edition 2009, reprinted 2011, 2013, 2015
10 9 8 7 6 5 4 3

Acknowledgments
Every effort has been made to trace copyright holders for previously published quotations. Please contact the publishers if you have any further information about unacknowledged quotation, which will be fully credited in the event of a reprint.
Unless otherwise stated, scripture quotations are taken from the Holy Bible, New International Version, copyright © 1973, 1978, 1984 by International Bible Society, used by permission of Hodder & Stoughton Publishers, a member of the Hachette Livre UK Group. All rights reserved. 'NIV' is a registered trademark of International Bible Society. UK trademark number 1448790.
Scriptures quoted from the Good News Bible published by The Bible Societies/HarperCollins Publishers Ltd, UK © American Bible Society 1966, 1971, 1976, 1992, are used with permission.
Extracts from The Living Bible copyright © Tyndale House Publishers 1971.
Scripture taken from The Amplified Bible, Old Testament copyright © 1965, 1987 by The Zondervan Corporation. The Amplified New Testament copyright © 1958, 1987 by The Lockman Foundation. Used by permission.
Scripture quotations from The Revised Standard Version of the Bible, copyright © 1945, 1952, 1971 by the Division of Christian Education of the National Council of the Churches of Christ in the United States of America, are used by permission. All rights reserved.
Scripture quotations from The Message. Copyright © 1993 by Eugene H. Peterson 1993, 1994, 1995. Used by permission of NavPress Publishing.
Extracts from the Authorized Version of the Bible (The King James Bible), the rights in which are vested in the Crown, are reproduced by permission of the Crown's patentee, Cambridge University Press.
'Jesus, you are changing me' by Marilyn Baker. Copyright © 1981 Authentic Publishing. Admin by Kingswaysongs, a division of David C Cook, tym@kingsway.co.uk. Used by permission.
'I will change your name' by D.J. Butler is copyright © 1987 Mercy/Vineyard Publishing. Administered by Song Solutions CopyCare, 14 Horsted Square, Uckfield TN22 1QG, info@songsolutions.org.
'Beauty for Ashes' by J. Danson-Smith. Copyright, used by permission of T.C. Danson-Smith. Poems by Gail Hutson. Copyright, used by kind permission.

A catalogue record for this book is available from the British Library

Printed and bound by CPI Group (UK) Ltd, Croydon, CR0 4YR

Beauty from Ashes

Readings for times of loss

Jennifer Rees Larcombe

To my friends Barbara and Violet

Without their help, encouragement and prayer, I could never have attempted to write this book

Acknowledgments

I would like to say a very large 'thank you' to all the friends who have allowed me to include in this book extracts from their letters or their own poems. They blessed me, and I pray that they will now bless other people.

Contents

Section 3: Dealing with the Lurkers

Section 4: The return of spring

Introduction

The day I began writing this book, my kitchen looked a mess! The walls and cupboard fronts were covered in scraps of paper, dusty and curling at the edges. For the last four years, I had been sticking them there at the rate of several a week. I started the habit on the day that I still think of as the worst day of my life. I had often said a prayer that sounded something like this: 'Lord, I could cope with anything—except that. If that worst fear of mine were ever to happen, I would be finished, finally and completely.'

But it happened. My worst fear became an ugly, messy reality. After that black day, I experienced all the bizarre stages of the grieving process—the shock, rage, depression; the 'why's, 'what if's and 'if only's, the panic attacks, the loneliness and that awful longing for death and oblivion. Surprisingly, though, I wasn't 'finished, finally and completely'! In fact, I discovered that God never allows us to go through our worst dread without giving us the strength to cope with it. More than that, he can actually use the experience to bless us profoundly. (Of course, I would have hit anyone who told me that when the mess was at its worst!)

As a trained counsellor, I understood all those ghastly stages of grief. Yet knowing what was happening to me did not help me much at all. It was those scraps of paper on my kitchen wall that kept me plodding along through my grief journey.

God has hidden, throughout the entire Bible, little phrases, promises and statements that I call the treasures of darkness (Isaiah 45:3). Reeling with shock and positively ill with grief, there was no way I could read long passages from the Bible.

But, when I woke early in the morning, feeling utterly lost and far too afraid to face the day, I would get up, make a mug of tea and sit in my rocking-chair. I couldn't concentrate enough to pray, I couldn't feel God's presence, but I used to sit gripping my Bible as if it were God's hand. Whenever I opened it and took a short peep inside, he seemed to cause one of these 'treasures of darkness' to catch my eye. It was uncanny the way they always seemed to speak directly to me about the way I felt that particular day. Because my brain was unable to hold on to anything for more than two minutes, I used to scribble them down on scraps of paper—and so they arrived on my kitchen wall. As I waited for the kettle to boil or the microwave to ping, I would read that day's acquisition over and over again, often feeling like a drowning man clinging to a lifebelt.

At first, of course, I did not realise that it is not enough to decorate the place with comforting little verses and nice promises from God; you actually have to believe them! For me, the 'crunch' came after several weeks of verse collecting. It was late at night and I was huddled under my duvet, on the sofa, quite overwhelmed by fear and an awful sense of desolation. I was too afraid to go to bed because there was a mouse in my wardrobe! That morning a friend had written to me saying, 'Take a look at Isaiah 54.' At that moment, reading the Bible was about the last thing I wanted to do, but anything was better than lying there, stiff with anxiety. So I found the place, and suddenly, this verse jumped right off the page.

Your maker is your husband.

ISAIAH 54:5

In other words, God was telling me that he was taking on the responsibility of caring for me, providing, protecting, cherishing and meeting all my needs, both practical and emotional.

I remember lying there, curled up tight as a ball, and realising I had a choice. I could either take God at his word and abandon myself to his love completely, or I could turn my back on him in disbelief.

'Take it or leave it!' I thought as I slowly crept out from under the duvet. I found a pen and paper and wrote the verse out, adding another from further down the page:

'Though the mountains be shaken and the hills be removed, yet my unfailing love for you will not be shaken nor my covenant of peace be removed', says the Lord, who has compassion on you.
ISAIAH 54:10

It felt as if I was making a very special pact with God as I stuck the paper in the place of honour over the kitchen sink. When I think back, I realise that the decision to believe it was the turning point in my recovery.

When I decided to write a book for people who are recovering from all kinds of loss, I realised that the best I could do was to share my 'scraps of paper' with them, hoping they would find them as much help as I had done. As I began pulling these scraps off the walls and cupboards, I remembered I also had a bundle of cards and letters that friends had sent me. I had stored them carefully away in the bottom drawer of my desk and soon I was sitting on the floor, with piles of paper laid out all around me. I felt as if I had discovered a gold mine!

Many described their own experiences or shared verses, quotations or coping strategies that had helped them. After making this discovery, I remembered all the other 'treasures of darkness' I had collected when my life had exploded into painful fragments on a previous occasion. Back in the 1980s I had been seriously ill with a brain virus that had left me in constant pain and, for eight long years, dependent on a wheelchair. God had undoubtedly mended my life that time, too, and soon another 'gold mine' of cards, verses and slips of paper was unearthed from a tea chest in the attic.

I finished this book four years after my worst fear became an ugly reality. Reading it again for this updated version, I realised what a long way I have come since then. I was obviously feeling so raw and vulnerable when I wrote it, and still needing a lot more healing. Perhaps if I were writing it now I would do so rather differently—but that would actually be such a pity. Books that are written by people years after some life-shaking event can often feel rather threatening to those still trudging through the rubble and ruins of their own catastrophe. When a writer is looking back from a distance, they can easily give the impression that God always felt close and that it was easy to overcome doubts, fears and regrets. Perhaps it is just very easy to forget how wounded, lost and confused we can feel at first. So, for that reason, I have resisted the temptation to make too many changes.

Yet, as I reread the book I remembered with a shudder just how difficult it had been to write, and how many times I had almost given up the struggle. Since it was first published, however, I have received shoals of letters from people who told me they had found it a help during their own 'grief journey'. Many said it felt like a friend walking along beside them. Those letters have made the pain of writing the book totally worthwhile.

My life has changed so much since those early days: I have founded a charity called Beauty From Ashes, which brings me into daily contact with thousands of other people walking the same 'valley of the shadow', and knowing them has enriched my life beyond description. God really is in the business of mending broken hearts and, although it is very difficult to believe this during the darkest times, it is possible to be happy again. Now, 13 years on from my own major loss, I find that I am happier and more fulfilled than I have ever been in my entire life. I live alone and my children are scattered all over the world, but real happiness does not depend on other people, what we possess, or even good health. I believe it comes from knowing you are loved by God right down in the core of your being—and revelling in the fact that he will never ever go away.

If your life has been shattered by some destructive experience, or you have lost someone you love, all I can say is, again, 'God is in the business of mending people.' He has done that for me twice now, and I've seen him do it for too many others to doubt his ability. The only thing he needs is for us to give him all the pieces of our broken hearts and lives, and to trust him to put us back together again in his own way and at his own pace.

The early stages

Where are you, God?

Who is among you who reverently fears the Lord, who obeys the voice of his Servant, yet who walks in darkness and deep trouble and has no shining splendour in his heart? Let him rely on, trust in, and be confident in the name of the Lord, and let him lean upon and be supported by his God.

ISAIAH 50:10 (AMP)

This was the very first verse to go up on my kitchen wall and I slapped it up there late in the evening of that dreaded day when I lost the person I love most in this world. I had rung a friend with the news long after her bedtime, but she had jumped straight into her car to bring me the verse written out on a card.

Some people say that they feel wonderfully 'carried' by God during those first few days or even weeks of loss, wafted along high above the earth and its horrible realities, on a golden cloud. I didn't. I felt nothing at all. There was no 'shining splendour' in my heart—or anywhere else for that matter. I spent my time mindlessly clearing out the garage, tidying the attic and sorting endless cupboards, late into the night. I did not cry, rage or worry about the future—until later!

When we are injured physically and pain becomes un-bearable, the body has a way of sliding into unconsciousness. Perhaps that numb feeling I experienced (and even the 'cloud nine' euphoria reported by others) is rather similar.

Our subconscious mind needs space to work through the implications of what has happened, so it switches off the emotions and renders us incapable of feeling anything.

This strange, detached state carries us over the worst part of our trauma but, while it saves us from feeling the bad emotions, it also cuts out the good ones. That is why it is often so hard to feel close to God after our lives have exploded. Prayer feels unsatisfying, reading the Bible is boring, and when we do pluck up enough courage to walk into church we might as well be singing nursery rhymes as hymns or praise songs to God.

When we realise that the 'shining splendour' in our hearts is missing, we panic. 'Just when I need God most, he's vanished,' we mutter furiously. But here's another of my kitchen verses:

Never will I leave you; never will I forsake you.
HEBREWS 13:5

That is a promise. We will always have his presence with us, but nowhere does he promise that we will always feel it. It is the fact of his presence that matters.

On a cold, grey, foggy day in January, no one doubts that the sun is shining up there in the sky, beyond the wintry clouds. We can't see it or feel its warmth but, even though our teeth are chattering and we have to switch the lights on at midday, we are still sure the sun is there, simply because it always is!

A prayer

Lord, I feel desolate. Most of what I valued is gone. Loss surrounds me—loss in all directions—leaving me cut off, alone, unprotected. All I can hear are the echoes of familiar voices and laughter from the past. The memories of all the things I wanted to do, places I

wanted to visit, people I wanted to meet, merely mock me now.
Worst of all, I feel I've lost you too, God. Where are you?

❦

God himself has said, I will not in any way fail you nor give
you up nor leave you without support. I will not, I will not,
I will not in any degree leave you helpless nor forsake nor let
you down (relax my hold on you)! Assuredly not!

HEBREWS 13:5 (AMP)

The Cinderella syndrome

The Spirit of the Sovereign Lord is on me, because the Lord has anointed me to preach good news to the poor. He has sent me to bind up the broken-hearted, to proclaim freedom for the captives and release from darkness for the prisoners… to comfort all who mourn, and provide for those who grieve in Zion—to bestow on them a crown of beauty instead of ashes, the oil of gladness instead of mourning, and a garment of praise instead of a spirit of despair.

ISAIAH 61:1–3

These verses meant so much to me that I put them up in the loo as well as in the kitchen. They were written 700 years before Jesus was born, yet they describe his mission so exactly that when he preached his first sermon he used them as his text, saying, 'Look, folks, this is me!' Well, not in quite those words! But he meant, 'I'm the hope of everyone who feels shattered, crushed, trapped and bereft. I can turn your tears into laughter.'

There is nothing so useless, bleak and dead as the ashes of yesterday's fire, and in the Bible ashes symbolise a sense of wretched desolation and loss. When something terrible happened, people would rip up their clothes in a great gesture of grief, wrap themselves in an old sack and scoop up handfuls of ashes to rub all over their heads.

Job, covered in painful and revolting sores and reeling from the loss of all his ten children, not to mention his business and reputation, crawled off to sit amid the rotting debris on the town's rubbish dump, telling his friends, 'I am reduced to dust and ashes' (Job 30:19).

Princess Tamar, King David's daughter, was little more than a child when she was sexually abused by her half-brother. In her distress, she put ashes on her head to express her inner desolation (2 Samuel 13:19–20).

On the other hand, brides and grooms both wore lovely crowns of flowers on their heads, and colourful clothes. So when God says he will give us a garland of beautiful flowers instead of ashes, he is promising to create a wedding dress from funeral black and a ballgown fit for a princess from Cinderella's rags.

We just have to go on handing him the ashes, handful by dismal handful, day by day—in naked faith, even when we can't see the beautiful garland he is holding, ready for us, behind his back.

One of the most precious cards I received during that early time came from an elderly friend. She told me how much this little poem had meant to her during many difficult years. When I look at her, I can definitely see the truth and reality contained in her poem.

'Beauty for ashes!' can He, can He give
When life's best years have gone—have passed away?
When cherished hopes, long held, no longer live,
And life seems now a drear monotony?

'Beauty for ashes!' Ashes! Yes indeed!
Ambitions, dreams and hope all shattered now:
Dearest ones gone, and none to care or heed:
Beauty for ashes? Can it be? And how?

'Beauty for ashes!' Can we thus exchange
These now cold embers of life's burned-out past
For beauty—beauty heavenly, wondrous, strange—
A beauty which throughout life's way can last?

Yes, for our ashes, He would have us take
Beauty—His own—each passing day to wear,
Till, in His likeness, satisfied, we wake,
And find new beauties, everlasting, there!

J. DANSON-SMITH

A prayer

Lord, right now I don't have the energy even to try to believe you can transform the blackened, charred ruins of my life into anything new or beautiful. But I want to want to believe it!

Wounded

I am poor and needy, and my heart is wounded within me.
PSALM 109:22

Thy name is as ointment poured forth.
SONG OF SONGS 1:3 (KJV)

What amazed me, as I sifted through all my 'kitchen verses', was just how many different metaphors the Bible uses to describe the way we feel when our lives are smashed. Walking in darkness, being reduced to ashes, trapped in prison, walking through a deep valley—hundreds more—but one of the most frequently used is the feeling of being wounded. Someone whose marriage broke up told me that she felt as if she had been brutally stabbed with a bayonet.

People whose lives have never collapsed often underestimate how 'wounded' we are. They urge us to 'forgive, put it all behind you', or 'keep praising Jesus', and even, 'you must just accept a new life now'. Of course, we all know these things are necessary but no one says that kind of thing to a patient in an intensive care unit just after a major car accident. While he is still struggling for survival, it would be too soon. We also need time to recover from emotional wounds, which are just as real, even though they are invisible.

When I visited the Ukraine, I bought a Russian doll in Kiev market. She now stands on my bookcase looking, at first sight, like a shapeless peasant in garish-coloured clothes. If, however, you unscrew her, you find another layer under the surface, then another and so on—level after level. I think we're all rather like her. The outside, physical part of us, which everyone sees, is only a fraction of the 'real us'. We all have many secret inner layers. When we are hit by some life-changing catastrophe, we are wounded in all these various areas of our personality.

Suppose you had a serious road accident. Your physical injuries would be obvious to everyone who saw you, but the 'layer' where you feel would also have been damaged. You might find yourself uncharacteristically emotional—weepy, fearful and astonishingly irritable for no apparent reason.

Your 'thinking' layer would also have taken a bad knock, as all your values, priorities and usual thought patterns re-organised themselves. New, negative thoughts might trouble you as an inner voice told you, 'You'll be nothing and nobody if you have to give up work… If you become a burden on your family and friends, they'll reject you… Now this has happened, you're finished for life.'

The area of your desires and motivation would also be devastated. All the goals you'd aimed at throughout your life could suddenly be unattainable.

The very core of you, your spirit, would probably be crushed and lacerated too. Your faith in God and his protective power and goodness might be badly dented as you asked yourself, 'Why, when I prayed for safety at the start of that journey, didn't God protect me?'

All these various layers of the Russian doll have to heal at their own pace and must be given time to do so.

I remember once, when I was very ill in hospital, the drugs were given intravenously via a drip. I used to lie watching that vital, healing liquid dripping from the bag suspended over my head, down the clear tube and straight into my arm, drip by precious drip. A visitor gave me another of my favourite kitchen verses: 'Thy name is as ointment poured forth.' (It says 'perfume' in more modern translations but ointment was often highly scented.) I used to lie there saying his name—'Jesus, Jesus, Jesus'—over and over again as I watched those life-restoring drips. More recently, when emotional pain has proved far more difficult to cope with than physical pain ever was, I have discovered that repeating his name works just as well.

'Jesus.' When we say that little word, we are invoking the most powerful name in the universe—the greatest possible source of healing.

He jests at scars that never felt a wound.
SHAKESPEARE (ROMEO AND JULIET)

What wound did ever heal but by degrees?
SHAKESPEARE (OTHELLO)

The grey cloud

All your waves and billows have gone over me, and floods of sorrow pour upon me like a thundering cataract. Yet day by day the Lord also pours out his steadfast love upon me.

PSALM 42:7–8A (LB)

A nurse who worked for months in a 'battle zone' hospital told me how hard it is for patients who have been injured by bomb blasts to pluck up enough courage to look at their wounds. Perhaps an arm or leg has gone but it is not until the bandages are taken off and the actual loss is exposed that the patient begins to realise what has happened to him. The moment when he sees the stump is a terrible one but very necessary for his recovery.

The numbness which, at first, 'bandages' our emotional wounds wears off eventually and we are hit by the realisation of just how much we have lost. Often the first thing we feel is an awful sense of sadness, like a heavy grey cloud, weighing us down.

It used to settle on me as I woke in the morning and it hung over me all day. Just now and again it lifted for an hour or so, letting me feel that I was recovering at last—and then down it would come again. Like King David, I remember wondering, 'How long must I wrestle with my thoughts and every day have sorrow in my heart?' (Psalm 13:2).

The most helpful thing anyone said to me at that time was,

'It will pass.' Of course, I didn't really believe them, but I clung to the hope all the same. And it did pass. Soon I was having alternate good and bad days; then, at last, I realised that the grey clouds were descending only occasionally.

But how long does it last? Usually longer than we think it will and a lot longer than our friends feel it should! While they are telling us we ought to be over it by now, that crippling feeling of sorrow can still take us by surprise.

A friend who had recently lost her husband once told me, 'There is no getting over sorrow, but there is a getting into it, and finding, right in the heart of it, the Man of Sorrows himself. No, you don't get over it, but you do get through it, right into the heart of God.'

Often, it is memories from the life that has gone that bring the clouds down round us. An old pop song played on the radio, the scent of a flower, or the discovery of a forgotten pair of wellies in the garden shed—all these can bring 'the light of other days around us' (to paraphrase the poet Thomas Moore) and cause an unbearable sense of loss. The only thing that ever helps me then is this verse:

Surely he hath borne our griefs, and carried our sorrows.
ISAIAH 53:4 (KJV)

I remind myself that Jesus really is walking along beside me and that he wants me to shift this crushing load over on to him so that he can carry it for me. So I say to him, 'Thank you for those times I'm remembering. They are good memories, but right now I can't bear the sadness they produce. So will you carry this for me?' It can be dangerous to bury memories but this is simply a matter of shifting them over on to Jesus, the grief-bearer. It always comforts me to realise that he was actually there when the memories were current events.

A prayer

Lord, it is so hard to believe 'it will pass', but please keep hope alive in my heart. Thank you that one day, you are going to overcome sorrow for ever. Amen

❦

Here [the Lord Almighty] will suddenly remove the cloud of sorrow that has been hanging over all the nations. The Sovereign Lord will destroy death for ever! He will wipe away the tears from everyone's eyes.

ISAIAH 25:7–8A (GNB)

— Day 5 —

Who cares?

You have seen me tossing and turning through the night. You have collected all my tears and preserved them in your bottle! You have recorded every one in your book.

PSALM 56:8 (LB)

Some people are so much better at crying than others! I'm sure God invented tears to give us a way of getting sorrow out of our systems, yet some of us are so embarrassed about 'breaking down'. Perhaps we were told, as children, 'Big boys don't cry', but tears that are not shed outwardly flow internally, rusting up the works and prolonging the grief.

'I seem to need to cry most of the time,' a friend told me, 'but other people get so embarrassed. They tell me not to cry—"It's not good for you, dear"—but I think they mean it isn't good for them!'

There is a limit to how much spilled emotion our friends and family can take. Most of us need to talk endlessly, going over and over the same memories and regrets until the patience of even our very best friends begins to run out—leaving us feeling isolated and bereft. 'Nobody understands—no one cares.'

Is it nothing to you, all you who pass by? Look around and see. Is any suffering like my suffering…?

LAMENTATIONS 1:12

I often used to hide my tears all day long from the family, because I did not want to add to their grief. Then, finally, in bed I would have a good long cry. But there is something awful about crying alone in the dark. All the pairs of arms that could be relied on to comfort in the past are missing. It was during one such night that the verse at the beginning of this chapter became one of my 'specials'. God hasn't gone. He isn't embarrassed or impatient; he doesn't shrug and say, 'She'll get over it soon—this is just a normal stage in the grieving process.' He actually cares about each individual tear.

And he doesn't mind how often I say the same thing: he always listens. It was when I had just about exhausted most of my friends with my need to talk that a scrap of paper arrived in the post one day. The person who wrote it obviously knew how I felt.

Could you just listen?

When I ask you to listen to me and you start giving me advice, you have not done what I asked. When I ask you to listen to me and you begin to tell me why I shouldn't feel that way, you are trampling on my feelings. When I ask you to listen to me and you feel you have to do something to solve my problem, you have failed me—strange as that may seem.

Listen! All I ask is that you listen, not talk or do, just hear me. Advice is cheap.

When you do something for me that I can and need to do for myself, you contribute to my fear and inadequacy. But when you accept, as a simple fact, that I do feel what I feel, no matter how irrational, then I can stop trying to convince you and get down to the business of understanding it.

Irrational feelings make sense when we understand what's behind them. And when that's clear, the answers are obvious and I don't need advice. Perhaps that's why prayer is so important for some people—God listens and stays with us but doesn't give advice all the time or try to fix things. God listens and gives us the power to work things through for ourselves, but I need you to be with me too.

So please, just listen. If you want to talk, wait a few minutes for your turn, and I'll listen to you.

DR RALPH ROUGHTON

The empty gap

When I look beside me, I see that there is no one to help me, no one to protect me. No one cares for me. Lord, I cry to you for help; you, Lord, are my protector; you are all I want in this life.

PSALM 142:4–5 (GNB)

I bring him all my complaints; I tell him all my troubles. When I am ready to give up, he knows what I should do.

PSALM 142:2–3A (GNB)

I put these words of King David up in my kitchen because of the phrase, 'When I look beside me...' When you lose someone you love, they leave a huge hole where you feel they still should be. You wake in the night and reach out for the familiar sleeping shape; the car seat beside you is empty; their armchair and place at table are unoccupied.

David had obviously discovered the secret of handling this 'empty gap' feeling. One day, he and his soldiers arrived home at the military camp where they had left their wives and children. A terrible scene of devastation lay before them. Raiders had ransacked the camp, burning, stealing, and kidnapping the women and children. No one was left.

So David and his men wept aloud until they had no strength left to weep.

1 SAMUEL 30:4

Faced with a disaster, most humans need to find someone to blame. So, once they had stopped crying, David's soldiers turned on him. In their frustrated fury, they were ready to stone him. He was as gutted as they were—he adored his family—so what did he do? Blame God?

David was greatly distressed because the men were talking of stoning him; each one was bitter in spirit because of his sons and daughters. But David found strength ['encouraged himself', KJV] in the Lord his God.

1 SAMUEL 30:6

The gap left by the people we love may never be filled by another human being, but I am convinced that it is possible to ask God himself to fill it. Of course, we want the warmth of human arms, but when we ask God to be our comforter he either lifts that feeling of desolation or he sends someone along at just the right moment. I've known him do that too often to think it is simply coincidence. Jesus did know what he was talking about when he said, 'You're blessed when you feel you've lost what is most dear to you. Only then can you be embraced by the One most dear to you' (Matthew 5:4, *THE MESSAGE*).

This old prayer comes from the book that helped me more than any other during the first four years of my loss (apart from the Bible, of course). It is an anthology compiled by Dr Leslie Weatherhead (*A Private House of Prayer*, Hodder, 1999).

I am not alone
By night,
Or by day,
Or by circumstance,
Neither in the silence,
Nor in the city's roar;
Nor as I lie
At the door of death,
Or stand on the
Threshold
Of a new life;
For thou art with me,
Around me,
Underneath me,
Bearing me up,
Giving me strength,
Calling me on.
I am not alone;
Thou hast been,
Thou wilt be,
Thou art
With me.
Lo, I am always in thy care.
Amen

SAMUEL F. PUGH

Beware of gloom spreading

No one came to my support, but everyone deserted me. May it not be held against them. But the Lord stood at my side and gave me strength.

2 TIMOTHY 4:16–17A

This 'grey cloud of sadness', with its sense of isolation and despair, is very hard to live through, but it is also hard to live with. When one member of a family, home group, circle of friends or colleagues is constantly wrapped in gloom after a personal loss, everyone else is affected.

'Since Dad lost his job, we've forgotten how to laugh in our house,' said one ten-year-old. An 18-year-old also told me, 'All the clocks stopped for Mum when Dad was killed, and the rest of us felt we had to put our lives on hold, too.'

Of course, it is wrong to press our feelings down deep inside ourselves, or to hide them behind a plastic smile that tries to fool everyone into thinking we are a triumphant, victorious, Christian martyr!

Denying our grief by pretending we are not hurt at all only delays it for a while, leaving it to erupt later in our lives in the form of depression or a physical illness.

Our need to express our feelings while not pulling others down by doing so is a dilemma as finely balanced as a seesaw. Perhaps we all need someone who is not too emotionally involved in the situation to whom we can regularly pour out our pain—a wise friend or compassionate counsellor. When we know we have a reliable outlet for our feelings, we won't have to dump them on everyone we encounter.

One evening, I caught my son looking anxiously at my face when he came in from work. 'Just checking on what kind of mood you're in,' he admitted. 'When the atmosphere round here is like a vault, I go to the gym.' Obviously the grey cloud is as infectious as the flu!

Soon after that enlightening conversation, I discovered another old prayer from the book that never left my bedside. I could not possibly count the times I've had to pray it ever since.

A prayer

O God... take from us all resentment and bitterness... Help us to bring happiness and peace to others, even when our own hearts are in turmoil.

Save us from spreading grief and sorrow, depression and despair. May we never sell our courage to buy sympathy. May we never sell another's good name to buy pity for ourselves. May we never blunt the truth about ourselves in order to excuse ourselves, or hide our motives from our scrutiny in a vain attempt to think more highly of ourselves than the truth warrants.

Show us that it is more enriching to show courage than to receive sympathy, even when no one suspects that there is anything to be courageous about. Show us that silent suffering, without bitterness or self-pity, can make us strong.

From advertising our self-martyrdoms; from blazing abroad our little sacrifices; from reciting our woes to others; O Lord, deliver us.

From yielding to melancholy moods that depress others; from the sullenness of temper that drives the sunshine from other faces; from

refusal to do battle with gloom and by that refusal to make life
rder for others; O Lord, deliver us.

May we be more ready to give to others our bread and our wine,
han to tell them of our hunger and our thirst.

Forgive us for all our failures and help us to start again each day
as thy loving sons and daughters, living in obedience and in trust.
Through Jesus Christ our Lord. Amen.

DR LESLIE WEATHERHEAD, *A PRIVATE HOUSE OF PRAYER*

The limbo world of change

I am the Lord, and I do not change.

MALACHI 3:6 (GNB)

There probably are some people who thrive on change, but most of us meet it with some trepidation! Even the kind of changes that you plan and look forward to, such as moving house, a new job or getting married, all cause stress because all change involves loss and adjustment. So it stands to reason that the kind of changes that you don't plan and definitely don't want will cause infinitely more stress.

The explosions that wreck our lives can blow us right out of the old familiar rut of our long-held attitudes, thought patterns, cosy little routines and daily activities. We are no longer the person we were before, nor are we yet the person we will become when the dust settles. In this unpleasant limbo we don't know who we are, where we fit in and what we are supposed to do next. A very horrid sensation indeed!

We spent our summer holidays in Scotland when I was a child. Up the hill, behind my grandfather's house, was a forest. We loved exploring the paths between the great trees that seemed to reach right up to the sky. I used to scare my little brother rigid with stories about the trolls, dragons and wicked fairies that watched us from the shadows: he always believed me! Our favourite spot was a huge granite rock in the centre of the forest. You couldn't see it from any of the paths because huge trees grew all round it but, cutting right into its pink granite heart, was a deep crevice. For many years this was our own secret camp.

When I had children of my own, I often told them about 'my forest' and one day I took them there. To my utter dismay, the Forestry Commission had felled the entire forest. All the familiar paths were lost, the great trees were gone, along with the spongy green moss, giant ants' nests, shy foxgloves and the pungent smell of pine needles.

A part of me had been desecrated and I just stood there gazing over the bald, scarred hillside, very near to tears. Then I saw my rock. There it stood, towering over the wreckage, conspicuous now that the trees were gone, but just the same as ever. As I stepped into the shadow of my familiar cleft, everything felt safe and normal once again.

When the landscape of our lives suddenly changes shape, like my forest, it is comforting to know that God, our 'rock of ages', never changes. As we squeeze ourselves into him—right to his very heart—the devastation that surrounds us ceases to be so frightening.

In 1847, when Henry Lyte was a curate in a little Devon fishing town, he developed a terminal illness. The day he preached his last sermon, he handed something to his churchwarden. It was a hymn he had just written—'Abide with me'—perhaps one of the best-known hymns of all time. With death so close, he knew all about the turmoil change produces, yet he wrote:

...Change and decay in all around I see,
O thou who changest not, abide with me.

I need thy presence every passing hour;
What but thy grace can foil the tempter's power?
Who like thyself my guide and stay can be?
Through cloud and sunshine, Lord, abide with me.

I fear no foe with thee at hand to bless;
Ills have no weight, and tears no bitterness.
Where is death's sting? Where, grave, thy victory?
I triumph still, if thou abide with me.

Hold thou thy cross before my closing eyes;
Shine through the gloom, and point me to the skies.
Heaven's morning breaks, and earth's vain shadows flee;
In life, in death, O Lord, abide with me.

❦

Jesus Christ is the same yesterday and today and for ever.

HEBREWS 13:8

Rejection

If it were an enemy that mocked me, I could endure it; if it were an opponent boasting over me, I could hide myself from him. But it is you, my companion, my colleague and close friend. We had intimate talks with each other and worshipped together in the Temple... My former companion attacked his friends; he broke his promises. His words were smoother than cream, but there was hatred in his heart; his words were as soothing as oil, but they cut like sharp swords. Leave your troubles with the Lord, and he will defend you.

PSALM 55:12–14, 20–22A (GNB)

Ouch! Poor David! He knew what a broken relationship feels like.

When you love and trust someone, and open every part of yourself to them—only to see them walk away, rejecting all you are and all you have—it hurts! It is no good trying to weigh grief by wondering if bereavement through death is more painful than losing someone through rejection or mental illness. Grief, whatever its cause, hurts.

But there is something about rejection that cuts right to the very centre of our being and rips out our confidence. It kills our self-worth and leaves us doubting the person we thought we were.

It also brings back memories of previous rejections: the parents who abandoned us, emotionally or physically; the 'best friend' at school, stolen by the 'new girl'; the first girlfriend who preferred someone else; and all those unsuccessful job interviews. Back come the memories, reinforcing the awful sense of being an unacceptable, unlovable, worthless person. Every memory of rejection sounds a note, and together they create an agonising discord that jars the whole system.

People who have always been loved—popular with peers, successful at work and sport—simply have no idea how it feels. Their tactless comments can add to our pain and make us feel even more marginalised. But there is someone who understands.

He was despised and rejected by men, a man of sorrows, and familiar with suffering.

ISAIAH 53:3A

His own brothers thought he was a liar (John 7:5); the crowds he had healed and fed deserted him (6:66); the nation he had come to save murdered him (19:15); and as he stood weeping over the city he loved so much, he said, 'How often I have longed to gather your children together, as a hen gathers her chicks under her wings, but you were not willing!' (Luke 13:34). Even his best friends fell asleep just when he needed them most, and one of them turned traitor and betrayed him. Yes, Jesus definitely knows how rejection feels.

A prayer

Lord, I feel like a conjoined twin who has just been severed without an anaesthetic. I'm only half a person now; the other half of me has wrenched itself away, leaving a great open wound. I don't want to go on living any more. No one can possibly understand how this feels—except you. Hold my hand, Lord. Get me through this; I'm too hurt to help myself. Thank you that you will never abandon me. Amen

❦

Can a mother forget the baby at her breast and have no compassion on the child she has borne? Though she may forget, I will not forget you! See, I have engraved you on the palms of my hands.

ISAIAH 49:15–16A

I have loved you with an everlasting love; I have drawn you with loving-kindness. I will build you up again and you will be rebuilt.

JEREMIAH 31:3–4A

Jesus, thou joy of loving hearts,
Thou fount of life, thou light of men,
From the best bliss that earth imparts
We turn, unfilled, to thee again.

BERNARD OF CLAIRVAUX

Turmoil

Desperate, I throw myself on you: you are my God! Hour by hour I place my days in your hand, safe from the hands out to get me. Warm me, your servant, with a smile; save me because you love me. Don't embarrass me by not showing up.

PSALM 31:14–17A (*THE MESSAGE*)

One morning, a card arrived from Lynne. Her own life was spinning with uncertainty and she wanted to share the verses that were helping her through it. Like so many of the treasures I'm sharing with you, Lynne's arrived just when I needed it most. That week I was facing the possibility of losing my home and the job I had enjoyed so much, and all kinds of major decisions had to be made without delay. My mind was in a complete spin—just when I most needed to think clearly. I was horribly conscious that if I made a wrong decision now it could affect me for the rest of my life. Every time I solved one of the many problems that threatened me, I seemed to create ten worse ones, and everyone I spoke to gave me conflicting advice.

To say I was in a 'state' is to put it mildly. The words on Lynne's card meant so much to me, they could well have come direct from heaven. 'Desperate, I throw myself on you…' Holding her card in my hand, I went and flung myself down in my rocking-chair, the place where I always go in the mornings to drink my first cup of tea and to be with the Lord.

'I am absolutely desperate,' I told him. 'So help me.' Noticing the words, 'Hour by hour I place my days in your hand', I decided to set my alarm clock, every hour on the hour, to remind me to come back here, to my rocking 'altar', to cast myself on his mercy. I can't say I prayed in words during the next few days. Whenever I heard that shrill bleeping, I was too agitated to think, let alone pray. So I just sat there for a few minutes, rocked a bit and then went back to whatever I had been doing—until the next time the alarm clock paged me.

I think what helped me was the act of flinging myself down in the rocking-chair. Praying in words would not have been the same; I needed a more tangible and dramatic way to express my longing to rush towards God as a small, bewildered child runs into its father's outstretched arms. My rocking-chair has certainly came to symbolise God's arms for me.

By the end of that alarm clock-punctuated week, a miracle had happened, but that is another story!

Here are more of my favourite 'worries' verses.

Therefore humble yourselves… under the mighty hand of God… Casting the whole of your care—all your anxieties, all your worries, all your concerns, once and for all—on him, for he cares for you affectionately and cares about you watchfully.

1 PETER 5:6–7 (AMP)

Commit your way to the Lord—roll and repose each care of your load on him; trust (lean on, rely on, and be confident) also in him and he will bring it to pass. And he will make your uprightness… as the shining sun of the noonday. Be still and rest in the Lord; wait for him and patiently lean yourself upon him.

PSALM 37:5–7A (AMP)

A prayer

Lord, I'm always screaming out to you—silently—imploring you to do something about the mess I'm in. But I know that prayer is not just telling you about my worries; it also means leaving you to sort them out. I find this 'trusting' bit of prayer so hard. Please help!

— Day 11 —

A strong hand to hold

In his hand is the life of every creature and the breath of all mankind.

JOB 12:10

The steps of a good man are directed and established by the Lord when He delights in his way—and He busies Himself with his every step. Though he falls, he shall not be utterly cast down, for the Lord grasps his hand in support and upholds him.

PSALM 37:23–24 (AMP)

For I, the Lord your God, hold your right hand; it is I who say to you, 'Fear not, I will help you.'

ISAIAH 41:13 (RSV)

These are three of my favourite verses about hands, but there are plenty more where they came from. When you lose someone you love, you don't have a hand to hold any more. I missed the big, kind, creative hands of my husband dreadfully at first; then I began to collect the many verses in the Bible that mention God's hands. How could anyone think that God is merely a distant, abstract force of good? Throughout the Bible we are told how his hands protect us; his eyes watch for our interests; his heart goes out to us; his shoulders are there for us to rest on and his face beams at us.

The God that the Bible describes wants to be utterly involved in the smallest detail of our lives and is always there for anyone who turns to him for protection.

One Sunday, I was sitting in church behind a couple, about my age, who held hands all through the service. I struggled hard to keep envy at bay. At the end of the service, the wife was in tears and I guessed they were in some kind of trouble. When the husband gently put his arm round her, my own sense of loss became unbearable. 'I haven't got a nice husband to comfort me when I feel bad,' I thought sourly, but instantly I sensed the Lord say, 'You've got me!' I remembered the verse that had become my centrepost—'Your Maker is your husband' (Isaiah 54:5)—so I stretched out my hand and gripped the invisible hand that I could only see and feel by faith. With my free hand I flipped through my Bible, looking for my favourite psalm.

Yet I always stay close to you, and you hold me by the hand… What else have I in heaven but you? Since I have you, what else could I want on earth? My mind and my body may grow weak, but God is my strength; he is all I ever need.

PSALM 73:23, 25–26 (GNB)

This reaching out of my hand towards his, and apparently gripping thin air, rapidly became a habit. I did it whenever I felt that ghastly 'alone' feeling spreading over me, or just as I walked into a room full of people or moved through the door to face a dreaded appointment.

Here is a fragment from a letter I found in another of the anthologies that became my 'crutches'. The letter was written to someone who lived 400 years ago, but it could easily have been written to me—or perhaps to you?

*Do not look forward to the changes and chances of this life in fear;
rather look to them with full hope that, as they arise, God, whose
you are, will deliver you out of them. He has kept you hitherto—
do you but hold fast to his dear hand, and he will lead you safely
through all things; and when you cannot stand, he will bear you
in his arms. Do not look forward to what may happen tomorrow;
the same everlasting father who cares for you today, will take care
of you tomorrow, and every day. Either he will shield you from
suffering, or he will give you unfailing strength to bear it. Be at
peace then, and put aside all anxious thoughts and imaginations.*

FRANCIS DE SALES, FROM *DAILY STRENGTH FOR DAILY NEEDS* (EYRE AND
SPOTTISWOODE, 1904)

Walking through
question marks

The black hole

He drew me up out of a horrible pit—a pit of tumult and of destruction—out of the miry clay (froth and slime), and set my feet upon a rock, steadying my steps and establishing my goings. And he has put a new song in my mouth, a song of praise to our God.

PSALM 40:2–3A (AMP)

I was driving along a busy bypass when I hit the 'black hole'. I wasn't thinking of anything much, just idly listening to a praise tape, when an enormous surge of painful indignation hit me. I 'killed' the music viciously and said such a rude word, my mother would have turned in her grave if she'd heard me.

'How could you?' I screamed. (Praying in a car is so satisfying —you can shout, scream and cry as loudly as you like and no one else hears you.) 'How could you stand by and let all this happen to me? Didn't I take the trouble to commit each area of my life to you every morning? You could easily have prevented this mess I'm in!'

This grieving business is such a strange kaleidoscope of emotions. One day you can feel as if God is your only protector and provider and the next he suddenly feels like your worst enemy.

I call this ghastly sense of disappointment with God 'the black hole'—the moment when you think, 'He's let me down! Either he's not as powerful as I thought he was or he isn't as loving as he's supposed to be.' The black hole is full of questions that don't have answers.

I stayed in my black hole for weeks, and my kitchen verses didn't make pleasant reading.

Why do I keep on suffering? Why are my wounds incurable? Why won't they heal? Do you intend to disappoint me like a stream that goes dry in the summer?'
JEREMIAH 15:18 (GNB)

O Lord, you deceived me, and I was deceived; you over-powered me and prevailed.
JEREMIAH 20:7

Then it gradually dawned on me that, while all these negative and angry verses were providing me with companionship in the black hole, if I wanted to get out I would need the help of some of the more positive bits of the Bible. That is when I wrote out the words at the beginning of this chapter and several others like it. I used to take one to bed with me at night and repeat it as I fell asleep, or mutter another under my breath as I walked the dog. I felt nothing as I parroted the words—they touched neither my mind nor my emotions—but, I suppose, saying them was an act of faith and gradually it began to have an effect.

I believe it is pointless to try to work your own way out of a black hole by struggling to understand the theology of suffering. We can never reach God by the limited ladder of human intellect but only by an irrational leap of faith. More than a hundred years ago, soon after the tragic death of her son, Hannah Whitall Smith wrote, 'Doubts are to be overcome not by reasoning but by faith. "I will believe; I choose to be-lieve" have been the weapons with which I have conquered in many a fierce battle. For the will has far more to do with our believing than most people think' (*God is Enough*, eds. Melvin and Halle Dieter, Zondervan, 1986).

Sometimes, waiting for God to explain why he has allowed our lives to collapse is the hardest thing he can ever ask us to do for him, because it requires more faith than preaching to millions or being thrown to the lions.

❦

I waited patiently and expectantly for the Lord; and he inclined to me and heard my cry.

PSALM 40:1 (AMP)

What happens inside the black hole?

We were so utterly and unbearably weighed down and crushed that we despaired even of life itself. Indeed, we felt within ourselves that we had received the very sentence of death, but that was to keep us from trusting in and depending on ourselves instead of on God.

2 CORINTHIANS 1:8B–9 (AMP)

The apostle Paul could understand why God had allowed his difficult experience because he was at the end of it, but it is not so easy when we are right in the middle of confusing problems.

Perhaps it's the sense of powerlessness that hurts the most, down there in the black hole. We feel we've lost control of our lives as every plan we make in order to extricate ourselves from our problems comes to nothing. Even prayer is useless because God seems deaf, blind and fast asleep.

We all like to feel we control our own destinies, but surely this sense of 'being in charge' is only an illusion?

Some years ago, I had a holiday on a small, unspoilt Greek island. Never having been fond of lying in the sun, I spent my time exploring the deserted beaches that lay in the folds of the rocky coastline. My favourite was actually a private bay, belonging to the millionaire who owned most of the island. He was building himself a splendid mansion at the top of the olive groves that circled the beach. Soon, I guessed, walls and stern notices would exclude people like me from his personal stretch of sand. However, all the activity was still focused on the rapidly rising palace, and the beach was still mine—except, of course, for the ants.

As I sat eating my lunch on the rocky bank that separated the olive grove and the sand, I noticed them scuttling importantly in neat lines between my crumbs and their underground city. They were totally absorbed in organising their miniature world, and there is no denying that ant achievements are phenomenal; but beyond the trees roared those huge earthmoving machines. Any day they would be down here, ripping apart the ants' lifework with one snap of their iron jaws. The millionaire must have his paved barbecue area and beachside pool.

I often think of those ants whenever I face the issue of who controls my life—me or God.

The following day, when I returned to the beach, a small boy of about six was just as absorbed by the ants as I had been. During the day he kept emerging from the olive trees to sit and watch their frenzied industry. Who was he? I wondered, and began to suspect that he was the son of the millionaire. My imagination kicked in and I soon had him going to his father and saying, 'Dad, I really love those ants on the beach. When the men start digging our patio, could you ask them to leave the bit of the bank where the ants live—so I can go on studying them?'

The father would have to be unusually indulgent to make my story possible, but I couldn't help thinking how dependent those ants were on the whim of that millionaire. One word from him and their world would be preserved or destroyed. The ants didn't realise that! They thought their future safety depended on their own frantic activity. They felt in control of their carefully constructed world, when really it was the millionaire, who was far too big for their comprehension, who was in charge.

Small and frail as ants, our only hope is to depend on God completely. The more we rely on him, the more he is able to do for us.

A prayer

Lord, all my props have been kicked away, one by one. I feel I am sinking into terrifying oblivion. I know that my only hope is to seize you with both hands. Help me, because I am so much smaller than I thought I was.

— Day 14 —

Knowing God

The Lord says, 'The wise should not boast of their wisdom, nor the strong of their strength, nor the rich of their wealth. If anyone wants to boast, he should boast that he knows and understands me, because my love is constant, and I do what is just and right.'

JEREMIAH 9:23–24A (GNB)

I could have sworn that today's verse (and yesterday's) had never been in my Bible before they jumped out at me, demanding to go up on my kitchen wall. Laid side by side on my fridge door, they helped me to understand some of the purposes God had up his sleeve for me. He definitely wanted me to depend on him more (2 Corinthians 1:8–9) but he also wanted me to know him better. Of course, I always thought I depended on him completely. When we are fit, fulfilled in a career, comfortably off and surrounded by the people we love, it is so easy to think that God is our security when actually our needs are being met in all these other ways. When all the props are knocked away and we find we only have God left, then we discover where our dependency lies!

But it is impossible to depend on someone unless you know them personally and feel certain there are no flaws in their character.

All the things Jeremiah lists can be lost in an instant through redundancy, accident, illness or the treachery of others. One hundred years from now, the only thing any of us will possibly be able to boast about will be our relationship with God—and that will continue for eternity.

To be honest, I've struggled all my life over believing that God could really love me personally. Because of incidents in my childhood, I have found it easier to believe he loves other, more deserving, people far more. Yet, in spite of the odd black hole, the greatest thing that has come out of my experience of loss is the final certainty that I am loved—loved just the way I am, and just because I am! When your need for God is paramount, that is when you discover the depth of his love and goodness.

Here is another 'treasure' from my 'gold mine' of cards—a snippet from Mother Julian of Norwich, written hundreds of years ago but still just as true:

The best prayer is to rest in the goodness of God, knowing that that goodness can reach right down to our lowest depth of need.

Of course, God isn't fair! Not in this life, anyway. Good, yes; loving, definitely—but not fair. He does leave the selfish and the mean to prosper and he does allow repeated disasters to wreck the lives of many delightful people. He doesn't appear to reward good behaviour or punish bad. It is in the next life that he promises to put the records straight.

This old hymn is one that became very special to me. It was written by a young man who suddenly became blind. His fiancée could not face life married to a disabled husband so she deserted him. Out of the pain of that experience, he wrote this:

O love that wilt not let me go,
I rest my weary soul in thee;
I give thee back the life I owe,
That in thine ocean depths its flow
May richer, fuller be.

O joy that seekest me through pain,
I cannot close my heart to thee;
I trace the rainbow through the rain,
And feel the promise is not vain,
That morn shall tearless be.

GEORGE MATHESON (1842–1906)

— Day 15 —

But what is God really like?

The Lord will make you go through hard times, but he him-self will be there to teach you, and you will not have to search for him any more. If you wander off the road to the right or the left, you will hear his voice behind you saying, 'Here is the road. Follow it.'

ISAIAH 30:20–21 (GNB)

'Your Christian faith must be such a help to you right now,' gushed a well-meaning friend during one of my 'black holes'. I smiled vaguely but thought, 'Actually all this would be far easier to accept if I didn't believe in a powerful God of love.' The black hole is such a huge crisis of trust that sometimes it would be so much simpler to give up the struggle to hold on to our faith when it doesn't seem to be doing anything for us.

While I found most of today's kitchen verses a great comfort, the first phrase stuck in my throat a bit. Does God really 'make us go through hard times'? I am now fully convinced that the faithful, loving person I have recently come to know, better than ever before, does not sit up in heaven planning nasty things with the intention of doing me good. Frankly, I wouldn't want to have anything to do with someone like that.

Yet I am sure he does allow us to be human. Human beings go through 'hard times' and God allows them because he wants to use them to change and enrich our lives. There is a verse that irritated me so much, I refused to put it on my kitchen wall: 'All things work together for good to them that love God' (Romans 8:28, KJV). Only when I began to see the good that God was achieving out of my mess was I finally able to stick it on the fridge door.

Perhaps the misery of the black hole is increased because many of us have a very distorted picture of what God is really like.

Melanie was married to a vicar and heavily involved in church activities when she discovered that he was having an affair with a member of the worship group. Soon afterwards, he left her, their daughters, his job and his faith. Melanie felt she had lost everything,

'But worst of all,' she told me, 'I lost God too.' During counselling, she realised that the loss of her husband reminded her of the way she felt as a child when the father she adored abandoned her and her mother, leaving them to face great hardship. Her father and her husband had been the two 'strong men' in her life, to whom she had looked for security and, without realising it, her mind began to mix them with her image of God. If they could treat her so badly, and even leave her, then so could he. Subconsciously she had transferred the way she felt about her husband and father on to God.

A question

Sit for a moment with your eyes closed and imagine yourself looking up into the face of Jesus. Ask yourself:

- Is he frowning at me in disapproval?
- Is he looking away—disinterested?
- Is he pleased that I am suffering?
- Is he so angry that he is about to hurt me yet again?

- Is he looking away, revolted?
- Is he smiling at someone more important over my shoulder?
- Is he actually not there at all, because he would rather be with someone else?

If you saw any of these nasty portraits of God, scrap them at once. They are false. Perhaps they remind you of the adults who were important to you in childhood but they are not really pictures of God at all. Ask him now to help you begin to see the real, genuine God that the Bible depicts. That is a prayer he will definitely answer with a 'yes', even if he does so very gradually.

How does God feel?

'Simon, Simon, Satan has asked to sift you as wheat. But I have prayed for you, Simon, that your faith may not fail.'
LUKE 22:31–32A

Do not gloat over me, my enemy! Though I have fallen, I will rise. Though I sit in darkness, the Lord will be my light.
MICAH 7:8

Of course, God took a huge risk when he allowed all this to happen to you. When life gets tough, some people reject him for ever. And how does he feel then?

If he really does love each of us to the point where he would die for each of us individually; if he really knows us so intimately that he counts the hairs on our heads (Matthew 10:30); if he really enjoys us so much that he sings over us (Zephaniah 3:17), he must feel terrible when we turn away in bitter disappointment.

But it is because he loves us so much that he is willing to risk losing us. He knows there are more 'treasures' to be found down in the dark mines of adversity than we could ever discover in the sunshine of an easy life. When you really love someone, all you want is the very best for them. Because God longs to load us with these extra-rich blessings, he allows the harsh situations that have the potential for producing them.

God's enemy, Satan, is hell-bent on hurting God by snatching away anyone God loves. Before Peter experienced the worst night of his life, Jesus told him that Satan had asked permission to try to destroy him. He very nearly succeeded: we all know the story of the crowing cock (Luke 22:61).

While we struggle through our grief and confusion, we may feel utterly alone, but, of course, we are not. The superpowers—the forces of good and evil—are ranged above us. Satan wants to push us into deserting God while God wants us to burrow deeper into his heart. Both sides wait for us to decide who wins the battle (Job 1:6–12; 2:1–6).

Because God is everywhere at once, he does not stand aloof, watching the battle from a vast distance. King David tells us that 'the Lord is close to the brokenhearted and saves those who are crushed in spirit' (Psalm 34:18). But how does he really feel when he sees the agony some of us grapple with?

Remember how Jesus felt when one of his best friends, Mary, turned on him because she felt he had let her down (John 11:32–35)? He didn't answer her questions or reproach her for lack of faith. All that mattered to him, as they stood by her brother's grave, was the way she was feeling. He saw her weeping and he was 'deeply moved in spirit and troubled', and he wept with her (vv. 33, 35).

We talk so glibly, these days, about 'feeling angry with God'. While it is far better to express our feelings than deny them, still we need to remember that the more a person loves you, the greater is your ability to hurt them. God's love for us is so enormous that the potential we have for breaking his heart is colossal (Psalm 78:40–41).

God is big enough to take our angry outbursts, but Paul tells us to get rid of our anger by the end of the day (Ephesians 4:26). It is the kind of hidden, simmering, grudge-holding rage that we hold on to for days that breaks God's heart.

A prayer

Lord, I'm sorry I have doubted you so often recently. Please forgive the things I've said to you and the times when I've been too angry to speak to you at all. I don't want to push you away like this, because where else can I run, and who else have I got left now? Hold me, Lord; I'm so afraid.

The valley of the shadow

Even though I walk through the valley of the shadow of death, I will fear no evil, for you are with me; your rod and your staff, they comfort me.

PSALM 23:4

Happy are those who are strong in the Lord, who want above all else to follow your steps. When they walk through the Valley of Weeping it will became a place of springs where pools of blessing and refreshment collect after rains! They will grow constantly in strength and each of them is invited to meet with the Lord in Zion.

PSALM 84:5–7 (LB)

One Easter, we went on a bargain package holiday to Greece. The hotel was by the beach and the weather was lovely but after a few days we longed to get away from the crowds. The English hotel receptionist described a lovely village, set in the mountains behind the resort. She showed us the footpath on the map and, taking a picnic lunch, we set off.

As we strolled through the olive groves that wrapped the foothills, my husband, a biologist, went into raptures over the spring wild flowers that grew profusely under the silvery trees.

Then, quite suddenly, everything changed. The path led us into a dark valley that climbed sharply upwards between towering rocks. A dirty, polluted stream trickled among the slimy stones, smelling like the sewer it obviously was, and making the path dangerously slippery. The cliffs were so high that they excluded the sun completely and the temperature dropped to a damp, chilly level.

No flowers grew down here in this dark place and the atmosphere was eerie and sinister. I would have fallen over many times if my husband's big, strong hand had not been there to grab me, and I kept thinking how frightened I would feel in this evil place without his company.

Whenever I read about the 'valley of the shadow of death' in the 23rd Psalm, I remember that horrible place, and I wonder if David was thinking about a similar ravine when he wanted to describe a state of grief and desolation. The only reason he managed to stumble through the darkness of his bad times was because he knew the Lord was with him.

When we had been floundering along for over an hour, we came out of the valley, just as suddenly as we had gone into it. Around us was spread an enchanted land. On a sunny mountain 'shelf', overlooking the blue sea far below, nestled an ancient village, its terracotta tiled roofs contrasting beautifully with the gentle greens of the surrounding meadows and orchards. My husband discovered four rare wild orchids; a lady with a face like a wrinkled brown walnut picked oranges for us from her tree; and a young 'Greek god', leading a market-laden donkey, showed us a far easier path back down the mountain.

There was nothing pleasant about the time we spent struggling up that striking valley, yet I still rate that day as one of the best in my life. The sheer nastiness of the valley only increased our enjoyment of the village at the top.

Even before I was out of my valley of grief, I began to feel sure that there was a new, richer and more beautiful patch of life waiting for me when I finally emerged from the shadows. I was right: it actually is possible to be happy again, and life, although different, can be full of sunshine and colour.

The Bible mentions these dark, lonely valleys a number of times, and also gives promises for those of us who are trudging through them.

I will court her again, and bring her into the wilderness, and speak to her tenderly there. There I will give back her vineyards to her, and transform her Valley of Troubles into a Door of Hope. She will respond to me there, singing with joy as in days long ago in her youth.

HOSEA 2:14–15 (LB)

A prayer

Lord, sometimes the mess my life is in really gets to me. But thank you that you are in the mess with me.

— SECTION THREE —

Dealing with the Lurkers

— Day 18 —

It's all my fault!

Have mercy on me, O God, according to your unfailing love; according to your great compassion blot out my transgressions. Wash away all my iniquity and cleanse me from my sin. For I know my transgressions, and my sin is always before me... Wash me, and I shall be whiter than snow... Hide your face from my sins and blot out all my iniquity. Create in me a pure heart, O God, and renew a steadfast spirit within me.

PSALM 51:1–3, 7B, 9–10

The grief journey is not a straightforward trudge from one side to the other. The Lurkers see to that! They are invisible bandits that lurk behind the rocks along the way, waiting to leap out on us at unexpected moments, bullying, harassing and generally adding to our misery. I mean, of course, those maverick feelings that 'good Christians' are not supposed to have—like anger, shame, fear and doubt. Just when we think we have conquered them, up they pop once again, wearing a slightly different disguise. Fortunately God knows all about 'Lurkers': the Bible is full of them, and also of ways to handle them.

There is a group of these Lurkers with names like Guilt, Shame, Remorse and Regret. Sometimes we know we are not to blame for what has happened but the Lurker called Self-Reproach keeps whispering, 'You ought to have... if only you hadn't... why didn't you...' These thoughts are only the grief talking. Ignore them: they soon pass.

But suppose it was our fault: we did cause the car crash; it was our affair that wrecked the marriage, our dishonesty or carelessness that lost us the job. When they have a good case against us, the Lurkers are relentless, but it was because Jesus wanted to give us the right to tell them to get lost that he died in agony on the cross. Sometimes we let these bandits torture us for years because we feel we deserve to be punished for what we did or failed to do. By listening to them, and letting them hurt us, we are actually saying to Jesus, 'Your death was a waste of effort as far as I'm concerned.' But Jesus wanted to take the punishment so that we could be free.

When your partner leaves you, on top of the pain of rejection you can also be haunted by a sense of humiliation and failure. It is easy for friends to dismiss this by saying, 'But it wasn't your fault, dear', but secretly we know we did not love as unselfishly as we should have done. We didn't always treat him (or her) as we wanted to be treated ourselves. Failing to love is a sin, however we may have been provoked. So the Lurkers have us for lunch!

The only sure way to deal with any of these Guilt-Lurkers is to tell them, out loud if possible, that you have told Jesus all about the things they are reminding you of and that he has taken all the blame himself on the cross and has forgiven you completely. Lurkers hate that kind of firm talk; but watch out, they usually come back to have another go when they think you are off your guard!

A prayer

Lord, if only I could put the clock back, I would do so many things differently. I can't rewrite the past but I can give it to you. Thank you that you stepped down into this world to take the blame for all I have done wrong. Thank you for dying in agony on that cross so that I can go free of punishment. I want to dump this load of remorse at the foot of your cross in this big black dustbin sack you have provided. I will now walk away free of the rubbish but with deep gratitude for what you have done for me.

The prickly hedgehog syndrome

Wicked people and liars have attacked me... They oppose me, even though I love them and have prayed for them. They pay me back evil for good and hatred for love. Choose some corrupt judge to try my enemy, and let one of his own enemies accuse him. May he be... found guilty... May his life soon be ended; may someone else take his job! May his children become orphans, and his wife a widow! ... I am poor and needy; I am hurt to the depths of my heart... Help me, O Lord my God; because of your constant love, save me! Make my enemies know that you are the one who saves me. They may curse me, but you will bless me.

PSALM 109:2, 4–9, 22, 26–28B (GNB, ABRIDGED)

Grieving people are often as prickly as hedgehogs because anger is a normal reaction to pain and deep hurt. Yet Christians often beat themselves into a lather of condemnation when an Anger-Lurker attacks. 'I ought to be loving, accepting and forgiving,' we tell ourselves, 'not fuming with rage like this.'

Sometimes there is a definite 'someone' to blame for our misery: the drunk driver who caused the accident, the man who raped us, the mum who deserted us. Sometimes, however, nobody caused the disaster, so instead we feel angry with the vicar for not bothering to call, the doctor for being unsympathetic, the sister-in-law who made the tactless remarks.

Of course, we don't always admit we are angry. Perhaps we were brought up to 'count to ten—and smile nicely'. So we give our anger a nicer name and say, 'I'm baffled, disappointed, sad, upset, cynical—but of course I'm not at all angry.'

Anger is not a sin but what is wrong is the way we sometimes handle it. We can hurt someone else by our anger when we let it out in words or actions, or we can hurt ourselves by burying it. Trapped inside us, it turns into bitterness, which can sometimes cause physical illness, depression, eating disorders, obsessions and phobias.

The only way we can prevent our anger from damaging anyone is by finding a safe outlet for it (sport, pounding dough, hammering nails) or, better still, giving it to God. That is what David was doing when he wrote today's verses. Have you ever thought of writing an angry psalm—and then setting light to it or flushing it down the loo? Putting the anger down on paper and then destroying it has a wonderfully cleansing effect.

Whether our misery was caused by one obvious person or the lack of concern of many, the only way to rob these culprits of their ability to harm us is by forgiving them. They can still hurt us but when we decide to spit out the anger, grudges and blame that we hold against them, we instantly break their power.

It is easy to write something like that but so very hard to do it. In fact, I have come to the conclusion that, when someone totally devastates your life, it is impossible to forgive that person, however hard we try or however much we may be urged to do so by our friends. Humanly it is impossible; our only hope is to ask Jesus to come into the centre of our pain, to melt it with his love and then to give us a new heart and his power to forgive.

A prayer

Lord, I can't forgive them. Forgive me for not being able to forgive and please come into my heart and forgive them through me.

The polluted spring

Elisha… was staying in Jericho… The men of the city said to Elisha, 'Look, our lord, this town is well situated, as you can see, but the water is bad and the land is unproductive.' 'Bring me a new bowl,' he said, 'and put salt in it.' So they brought it to him. Then he went out to the spring and threw the salt into it, saying, 'This is what the Lord says: "I have healed this water. Never again will it cause death or make the land unproductive."'

2 KINGS 2:18–21

This little story has been a profound help to me. Jericho's water supply was contaminated, causing disease and death to both people and animals. In those days, communities could be completely destroyed by polluted wells: this was a danger-ous situation. Yet one handful of salt sweetened the water and brought life and health to a whole town.

I always think of the human spirit as a deep well, hidden inside us. Keeping it uncontaminated is as vital to the health of the personality as pure water was to Jericho. Yet anger, whether it is the noisy or the buried kind, can so quickly poison our spirit. Perhaps that is why the whole business of forgiving is so important, and yet so difficult.

We can make that decision to spit out the anger and breathe in the forgiving grace of Jesus, and we feel, 'That's a good job done.' Then, the next day, we can be washing up or driving to work and we suddenly think, 'But why did she say that to me? How could he have done that?' and suddenly we are overrun by Lurkers as all the same old angry thoughts come crowding back. We think, 'I've failed. I haven't forgiven after all.' But we have! It is just that forgiving means going through this 'spitting out and breathing in' routine whenever the angry thoughts trouble us. That may mean doing it many times a day, perhaps for the rest of our lives.

Because I was brought up never to show my anger, if something made me mad I'd smile sweetly, but under the surface my resentment would bubble away for hours. While I might have managed to hide it from the person who had upset me, anger had a way of spurting out at someone else altogether. Or my moody silence made everyone around me tense or miserable, contaminating everyone I encountered. I would soon find I was feeling uncomfortable with God as well. I'm learning now, as soon as I realise 'my well is poisoned', to ask the Lord to throw in a handful of salt before I cause any more damage.

When I remember first thing in the morning, before any Anger-Lurkers have had time to attack me, I also ask the Lord to throw some salt down my well. Prevention is better than cure!

A prayer

Lord, help me to see what it really means to have you living in me. You feel through my emotions, you hurt in my body: these things that they do to me, they do to you too. You say that the insults that they hurl at me have fallen on you. When they smash my life, they smash your life, too. When they steal my good name, they steal your honour, too. I know you feel angry for me and will fight on my behalf. Help me to rest in that fact. I want you to be angry with them, punish them, make them sorry; but when those men were hammering nails through your hands you prayed for their forgiveness. Please teach me how to forgive like that!

Where do you run?

You are my place of safety when trouble comes.
JEREMIAH 17:17B (GNB)

Fear is another of the Lurkers that dog our path through grief.
It takes so many forms, from a slight loss of confidence to a
paralysing anxiety state; chronic butterflies in the tummy to
major panic attacks. Again, Christians find fear demoralising
because we feel we ought to trust the Lord for everything and
bounce along victoriously—so we feel like frauds when an
unexpected Lurker suddenly trips us up.

Holidays, during the grief journey, are something of a mixed
blessing. You badly need a chance to get away and look at
your changed life from a distance, but going on your own,
when you have been one half of a couple, can intensify your
loneliness—even if you go with friends. The usual busyness of
everyday activities, which take your mind off your pain, is also
missing, and memories of past holidays confront you round
unexpected corners, robbing you of present enjoyment.

I went to Donegal in Ireland for my 'first', and I have to
confess, I didn't cope very well. One afternoon I left the kind
friends who had taken me on the holiday and went for a walk
alone. It was a perfect autumn day and I should have been
revelling in the view as I tramped across the hillside, but so
many uncertainties would be facing me when I arrived home

that I was simply trying to walk off the fear that walled me in on every side.

'Please, God, talk to me,' I muttered. 'Just when I need you most, I can't feel you're there any more.'

Suddenly, I realised I was not alone on the hills. Three farmers with petrol cans were spaced out across the hillside, setting light to the gorse bushes. Obviously they wanted to improve the grazing for their sheep but the effect was dramatic as flames leapt from one clump to the next, driven by a stiff wind.

Then I saw the rabbit. It ran, terrified, from the clump of gorse nearest to me. It had probably lived in a nice little burrow under the tangled black stalks all its life. Now it darted towards another clump where, perhaps, its aunts or cousins had always lived, obviously hoping for shelter; but another wall of flames sent it dashing back again. Frantic, it darted in all directions. The familiar landmarks and safe hiding places it had known and depended on all its life suddenly looked different and threatening, and some had disappeared altogether. 'Poor thing,' I thought. 'That's exactly how I feel! My life's all loss, change and threat, too, and I just don't know where to run either.'

One of the farmers had a gun and, catching sight of the helpless rabbit, he took aim. Just then, right in the middle of an open stretch of grass, the rabbit found a large hole. It was obviously not a familiar burrow or he would have made for it earlier, but he disappeared into its comfort and shelter just in time. As I walked back to join my friends, I realised God had used that rabbit to speak to me.

A prayer

Lord, everything in my life has 'gone up in flames'; all my little securities have gone, and people I relied on have let me down. I just don't know what to do for the best. I know that you are my place of safety at a time like this. So I choose to believe that you know what you are doing with my life and I seek shelter in your promises.

❦

'For I know the plans I have for you,' declares the Lord, 'plans to prosper you and not to harm you, plans to give you hope and a future.'

JEREMIAH 29:11

But how do you know what to do?

Each morning I will look to you in heaven and lay my requests before you, praying earnestly… Lord, lead me as you promised me you would; otherwise my enemies will conquer me. Tell me clearly what to do, which way to turn.

PSALM 5:3, 8 (LB)

O my Strength, I watch for you; you, O God, are my fortress, my loving God. God will go before me.

PSALM 59:9–10A

'I will lead my blind people by roads they have never travelled. I will turn their darkness into light and make rough country smooth before them. These are my promises, and I will keep them without fail.'

ISAIAH 42:16 (GNB)

It often seems unfair that, just when we are trying so hard to handle our grief, we also have to make all kinds of major decisions:

* Now I've lost my job, what shall I do about finding another?
* How do I fill my time now I'm retired?
* Do I try this new medical treatment or let things take their course?

- This house is too big now, but should I leave all my friends and move nearer my daughter?

So it goes on, and even when friends tell us soothingly to wait a bit before rushing into anything, we still turn the possibilities over in our minds endlessly.

I am sure there must be people who actually hear an audible voice from God telling them specifically what to do, but it would still take a lot of faith to act on instructions instead of thinking that the voice was imagined.

Others claim that a Bible verse jumped out at them, but it is hard to find a passage that says, 'Thou shalt live in Devon' or 'Thou shalt not live in Kent'!

Once, when I was in a real quandary, I went to a friend with a list of six possible courses of action, all typed out on a piece of A4 paper. He questioned me in depth about each one until I protested tearfully, 'All I want to do is what the Lord wants me to do, so why doesn't he just tell me?'

My friend smiled and said, 'Supposing you were sure that the Lord was happy for you to do any of these things, which would you like to do most?'

'Oh, that one,' I replied without hesitation, pointing to number three on the list.

'Then try that first,' he suggested. 'Seeing that your greatest desire is to do what pleases God, he will definitely stop you if he sees you heading the wrong way. He doesn't usually shout his orders to us while we are standing still, but if he sees us moving in the wrong direction, he has all kinds of subtle ways of blocking our path. If he does that to number three on your list, then try your next favourite option, and so on down your list.'

God, who understands the erratic emotions and helpless vulnerability of grief, loves us far too much to let us down at a time like this. One of my mother's little sayings went like this: 'The God who taught me to trust in his name would not have brought me thus far to put me to shame.'

This little quotation came inside another of my gold-mine cards:

I know the immovable comes down,
I know the invisible appears to me,
I know that he who is far
Outside of all creation
Takes me within himself and
Hides me in his arms.

ST SYMEON

A prayer

Lord, I know I can count on your 'goodness and mercy following me all the days of my life', but please help me not always to want to see them in advance.

Fear of the future

'Listen to me... you whom I have upheld since you were conceived, and have carried since your birth. Even to your old age and grey hairs I am he, I am he who will sustain you. I have made you and I will carry you; I will sustain you and I will rescue you.'

ISAIAH 46:3–4

'But how will I cope when I'm old and all alone?' Have you ever woken at five in the morning and been attacked by that kind of Lurker?

It was 1978. Our six children were all squashed into the church pew next to me but I wasn't concentrating on the service. We were facing a major family problem. My mother was no longer able to cope on her own but she loathed the idea of 'a Home'. If she lived with us, she would need our sitting-room as a bedroom, confining the rest of us to the kitchen. Would that be fair on the children—or on me, for that matter?

We had put the situation to the children over breakfast and asked them to join us in praying about it. Sarah, our eldest, was flipping idly through my Bible, obviously bored by the service. Suddenly she stopped, rigid with interest. From her pocket she produced a pencil stub; carefully underlining a few words, she passed me the open Bible.

If anyone does not take care of his relatives, especially the members of his own family, he has denied the faith and is worse than an unbeliever.

1 TIMOTHY 5:8 (GNB)

Sarah had never felt God speaking to her directly before, and on the way home she said, 'It felt as if he wrote those words just for me! Surely, Mummy, that's our answer?'

And for us it was. My mother lived with us until her death. I am certainly not suggesting it is right for all families to have their elderly relatives with them: other ways of caring may be far better and what blesses one family could kill another. God is simply telling us he holds us responsible for the emotional and physical well-being of our relatives.

In my Bible, that verse still bears the marks of Sarah's pencil and, when I noticed it again recently, I thought, 'If God tells us to care for the members of our families, then he will definitely do the same for his family. And we are his family.'

Pointing to his disciples, he said, 'Here are my mother and my brothers. For whoever does the will of my Father in heaven is my brother and sister and mother.'

MATTHEW 12:49–50

To all who received him, to those who believed in his name, he gave the right to become children of God.

JOHN 1:12

On the cross, just before he died, Jesus was concerned for his mother's future and gasped out his instructions for her protection. If he sees us as special members of his family, too, then how can we possibly doubt that he will be just as concerned to provide for us?

One of the many things I realised, during my difficult years of adjustment, was that God wants us to think of him as even more closely related to us than a child, brother or sister—and he wants me to think of him as a perfect husband (Isaiah 54:5). So I wrote out the words of the old marriage service and stuck them up on my wall, too. He is a faithful husband who never breaks his promise. He wants to make this sacred vow to you as you read these words.

A promise

I, Jesus Christ, take thee, _____ *, to my wedded wife;*
To have and to hold from this day forward;
For better, for worse;
For richer, for poorer;
In sickness and in heath;
To love and to cherish;
Till death us do (permanently unite)
according to God's holy ordinance;
And thereto I plight thee my troth.

Money worries

And God is able to make all grace abound to you, so that in all things at all times, having all that you need, you will abound in every good work.

2 CORINTHIANS 9:8

And my God will meet all your needs according to his glorious riches in Christ Jesus.

PHILIPPIANS 4:19

When I realised the significance of the 'alls' in these verses, I underlined them heavily before they went up on the wall. Loss of a job, person or health often presents us with money worries. I've already told you how anxious I became over money, but since I made that deliberate decision to 'cast my burden upon the Lord', there have been numerous occasions when big bills have arrived at exactly the same time as some unexpected windfall which just covered them perfectly.

Until my loss, I never had much to do with money. I was married to an efficient husband and left all that to him. So my son had to rush home from university and help me open my first bank account—and show me how to use a plastic card. My learning curve was steep but two of the things that the Bible teaches us about money have been a real help to me.

The first is the example of the widow who gave all she had (Luke 21:2–4). When our financial security is threatened, our instinct is to hoard what we have, but Jesus tells us, 'Give, and it will be given to you… For with the measure you use, it will be measured to you' (Luke 6:38). God gives to us as he sees us give to others.

Grief, shock and loss have a way of acting like a thick blanket, blinding us to the needs of others. We feel we just can't cope with their pain on top of our own. Yet if we can make ourselves peep out of our 'blanket' just long enough to notice their misery and do something to help, it not only brings light into our darkness but it also seems to increase God's grace towards us. Try the principle out for yourself. Next time you have a financial need, give to someone else!

'If you give food to the hungry and satisfy those who are in need, then the darkness around you will turn to the brightness of noon. And I will always guide you and satisfy you with good things. I will keep you strong and well. You will be like a garden that has plenty of water, like a spring of water that never runs dry.'

ISAIAH 58:10–11 (GNB)

The other principle I cling to is simply this: God keeps his promises!

Fear the Lord, you his saints, for those who fear him lack nothing. The lions may grow weak and hungry, but those who seek the Lord lack no good thing.

PSALM 34:9–10

'Do not worry, saying, "What shall we eat?" or "What shall we drink?" or "What shall we wear?" … Your heavenly Father knows that you need them. But seek first his kingdom and his righteousness, and all these things will be given to you as well.'

MATTHEW 6:31–33

During all my life, I have never once seen anyone who entrusted themselves and their families to God face real hardship. They may not have become millionaires but, surely, having enough each day is to be rich?

A prayer

Lord, I put into your hands, once again, all my finances. I know you have promised to take care of me and all that concerns me, but there is a part of me that wants to be in control and to find ways of meeting my own needs. I find it so hard to rely on you and to feel sure that you can and will provide for me. I want to believe; please increase my faith.

The worst Lurker of the lot!

The cords of death entangled me, the anguish of the grave came upon me; I was overcome by trouble and sorrow. Then I called on the name of the Lord: 'O Lord, save me!'

PSALM 116:3–4

Death. It's the subject we never talk about, yet the fear of it haunts most of us. However strongly we believe in heaven, and even when we know for sure that this life is merely a brief prelude to our real existence, the actual prospect of dying is frightening. I have had three close encounters and, although they have altered my values and priorities, I still shudder when I think of them. Perhaps you too have had 'a close shave'—a heart attack, accident or stroke? Or maybe you have been given a harsh diagnosis. You may feel able to face death for yourself but you can't bear the prospect for the people you will leave behind. I remember that the hardest thing for me was deciding whether I could trust God to take care of my children if I should die. It is so much easier to trust him for ourselves. Perhaps the hardest of all is to watch someone you love gradually slipping away from you.

Fears are normal but, like mushrooms, they grow bigger in the dark. We let in the light when we dare to talk about how we feel.

Dick had been in hospital for three weeks undergoing extensive surgery. He never asked the medical staff for their prognosis and he avoided the subject when his family and friends visited him. It was only in the night that the nameless, unexpressed fears loomed very large and his body felt far too tense for sleep.

One day another patient stopped by his bed for a chat. 'I hear we're both fighting the big C,' he said with a rueful smile. An hour later they were still talking. For Dick, the relief of putting his feelings into words was enormous.

When Dick was sent home, however, a wall seemed to have developed between himself and his wife. Just when they needed each other most, they felt miles apart. Dick did not know how much the doctors had told her and she wondered if he realised how ill he was. It was not until a wise Macmillan nurse gently helped them to share how they each felt that this wall was demolished.

We long to spare our families pain but, by keeping silent, we increase rather than lessen it.

One thing we can be sure about: we are never alone when we have to take that leap off this tiny, restrictive planet into the freedom of eternity. We are always met, welcomed and escorted. Many people who know the Lord, when reaching the point of death, suddenly look up and smile as if he had just arrived to take them home.

I eagerly expect and hope that I will in no way be ashamed, but will have sufficient courage so that now as always Christ will be exalted in my body, whether by life or by death. For to me, to live is Christ and to die is gain. If I am to go on living in the body, this will mean fruitful labour for me. Yet what shall I choose? I do not know! I am torn between the two: I desire to depart and be with Christ, which is better by far; but it is more necessary for you that I remain in the body.

PHILIPPIANS 1:20–24

A prayer

Lord, this world is not much fun. I've had enough of it really, yet life down here is all I know. Walking right up to the edge of something so very different makes me feel afraid. I know I have to leap off into the unknown, but that means wrenching myself away from the people I love so much. Please, when the moment comes, hold me tight, but hold them even tighter.

Stings and scratches

We take captive every thought to make it obedient to Christ.
2 CORINTHIANS 10:5B

Have you ever wished you could unscrew your head and take it off for a while? I have! It's the negative chatter, which goes on all the time, that I find so exhausting. I can be talking to a friend, watching TV or working at my computer with one part of my mind while another is being bombarded by thoughts that go round and round like a cassette stuck in a tape player.

'You'll never cope with this job… You're too old… out of touch… past it… You're such a failure, God couldn't possibly use you.'

I think Job knew what it feels like, when he said, 'I have no peace, no quietness; I have no rest, but only turmoil' (Job 3:26).

We all have our own set of tapes that secretly play inside our heads; the problem is finding the 'off' button.

I can vividly remember a summer day I once spent with my two-year-old granddaughter, Millie. After lunch, we decided to go on a dragonfly hunt and set off along the footpath that led to the pond, but we soon discovered that it was blocked. Heavy rain had battered down the stinging nettles and brambles, leaving them lying across the path. Millie stopped. Her bare legs looked vulnerable in their small red wellies.

'I don't like scratchy stings,' she announced nervously.

'Come on, let's stamp on them,' I replied. 'They won't hurt when they're under our boots.'

'Stamp, stamp, stamp!' we shouted in unison as, one by one, the weeds crunched beneath our feet. Millie's chest was thrust out importantly as her little legs vanquished each foe. By the time we reached the dragonfly pond, she looked positively power-crazed!

Later, as I drove home round the M25, the usual mental mutterings began again. 'These thoughts scratch and sting like the wretched brambles and nettles,' I told myself crossly. 'But perhaps you just have to stamp on them, one by one, like we did on the footpath.'

Maybe each mental 'stinging nettle' faces us with a choice. We can listen to the thought and let it sting us as we examine it from all angles, or we can stamp on it instantly by choosing to believe one of God's promises. For instance: 'I refuse to believe I am worthless; God says I'm the apple of his eye' (see Deuteronomy 32:10); 'I'm not going to fail because I can do all things through Christ who gives me strength' (see Philippians 4:13).

Of course, these negative thoughts are normal after any loss, but if we do nothing about them they develop into a set way of thinking, an attitude to life, that begins to dominate us. So I tried to form a new habit. The moment I caught myself thinking a negative thought, I refused it. If I was on my own, I actually stamped on it as if it really were a stinging nettle. I am convinced God can change our thought patterns as effectively as he can change everything else about us, but he does need our help. The 'off button' that silences that inner chatter is the decision to take God at his word.

Even when we are too weak to have any faith left, he remains faithful to us and will help us, for he cannot disown us who are part of himself, and he will always carry out his promises to us.

2 TIMOTHY 2:13 (LB)

A prayer

Lord, why am I so horrible to myself? The voice in my head is so abusive. Sometimes it sounds like that awful teacher at school, my mum or some other echo from the past. Please, Lord, change the way I think about myself. I've never liked this person who is me very much, but help me to see myself as you see me; help me to speak to myself lovingly—building myself up with encouragement rather than always putting myself down.

I want out!

My heart is in anguish within me; the terrors of death assail me. Fear and trembling have beset me; horror has overwhelmed me. I said, 'Oh, that I had the wings of a dove! I would fly away and be at rest—I would flee far away and stay in the desert; I would hurry to my place of shelter, far from the tempest and storm.'

PSALM 55:4–8

It was Boxing Day afternoon when, like David in this psalm, I 'wanted out'. Not having any dove's wings handy, I got into the car and drove to a straight stretch of the bypass. Aiming straight for a distant tree, I put my foot down hard on the accelerator. Perhaps it was the thought of the suffering I would bequeath to others that, just at the last minute, stopped me.

Living through grief is such a hideous experience that most of us long for a quick way out. A surprising number of us consider suicide. Other people who have only been social drinkers begin to use alcohol as a way of surviving the long, empty evenings. Casual relationships, video nasties, obsessive involvement with the Internet, comfort eating, compulsive busyness and spending money we don't have—there are so many ways of running away from the pain. Then, so often, we find that our method of escape has become a problem itself.

We can even use God as a 'way out'. We start waving our faith in his face, demanding healing or some other supernatural 'fix' for our problem, as if he were a magician with a wand. Of course, he has the ability to do anything we ask but sometimes he has his reasons for not doing so. Allowing him to know best is a hard but vital part of our relationship with him.

Was it this 'stop the world, I want to get off' feeling that Jesus was experiencing when he said in Gethsemane, 'My soul is overwhelmed with sorrow to the point of death... My Father, if it is possible, may this cup be taken from me' (Matthew 26:38–39)? At least he understands how we feel.

God promises us, 'When you pass through the waters, I will be with you; and when you pass through the rivers, they will not sweep over you. When you walk through the fire, you will not be burned; the flames will not set you ablaze' (Isaiah 43:2). He promises to walk with us through the floods and fire, from one side to the other, but he doesn't say he will spirit us out of them halfway through.

Here is an old hymn I would often sing to myself on bad days.

When through fiery trials thy pathway shall lie,
His grace all-sufficient shall be thy supply,
The flame shall not hurt thee, his only design
Thy dross to consume and thy gold to refine.

The soul that on Jesus has leaned for repose
He will not, he cannot, desert to its foes;
That soul, though all hell should endeavour to shake,
He never will leave, he will never forsake.

RICHARD KEEN (FROM *RIPPON'S SELECTION*, C.1787)

A prayer

Lord, why do I wake up each morning when you know I would prefer never to wake up again? I don't want to live any more—not this kind of life, anyway. All that I have lost has robbed me of all enthusiasm for life on this planet. I know you are with me in all the mess down here, but I would much prefer to be with you in heaven. Help me to be more like Jesus when he wanted to escape. He said, 'Yet not as I will, but as you will' (Matthew 26:39).

❦

'Be strong and courageous. Do not be afraid or terrified because of them, for the Lord your God goes with you; he will never leave you nor forsake you.'

DEUTERONOMY 31:6

The God who sings

The Lord your God is with you, he is mighty to save. He will take great delight in you, he will quiet you with his love, he will rejoice over you with singing.

ZEPHANIAH 3:17

One of the special things that you gain when your life crashes is the knowledge of who your friends really are. I can't count the times when the phone or the postman has brought a message from a friend that was exactly what I most needed to hear. Perhaps it is as we pray for others that the Lord shows us what they need.

During the time when I was plagued with suicidal thoughts, I had a letter from Jane Grayshon. She has been close to death several times, has undergone many operations and lives with severe pain. She has also shared her faith and her humour in books that have blessed many of us.

One night she could not sleep for pain and, between morphine injections, she wrote me this remarkable letter, knowing nothing about my dark thoughts—or my rocking-chair. Obviously the letter is personal, but with her permission I think it is well worth sharing with other grief travellers.

Dear, dear Jen,

I have carried you around in my heart every single day, holding you before the Lord. I feel as if I might understand just a tiny bit about the intense vulnerability you must feel, to which the natural reaction is, quite honestly, to wish for heaven.

Jen, bin this if it doesn't apply, but daily I'm so alongside you in the utter struggle of: 'Lord this is intolerable—the cost of being alive is too high; I can't muster the courage to want to go on.'

(Then Jane quotes from the book she had just finished writing, *Treasure of Darkness*, published by Hodder and Stoughton.)

'When God hits our strength and makes us weak, we are hurt and angry and mystified and many other things. But eventually, as we are ready to take his hand and accept his touch, we discover the blessedness of being stripped bare before him. Vulnerable, weak, poor and afraid, we come to him.'

And then, in my book, I go on to imagine his acceptance of us, and the reason I'm writing this to you, Jen, is that this is my longing, my prayer for you. I believe that your heavenly Father looks upon you and I can see his eyes crinkle with the lines of deep, unfathomable, patient love which melts your shame and draws you closer. I don't mean closer to heaven, I mean closer to him while you're on earth.

I pray that here, today (each day), you'll be able to see him smile on you with a delight which is genuine. He's stretching out his arms with the invitation which welcomes you before you've even arrived.

Now, he lifts you gently on to his lap. Like a mother, he enjoys rocking you in his rocking-chair, while you nestle into his arms, enfolded in his strong gentleness.

May you listen to his heartbeat and be reminded of that pulsating life which has fed you since you were being formed in your mother's womb. May you hear him humming a tune, his song, a song of contentment, because he has you where he wants you. (I don't understand this but I sense it very strongly—he has you where he wants you.)

Most of all, Jen, may you feel his breath fall upon your forehead. And may you enjoy it. (Again, the human bit of me wants to shriek, 'How can she enjoy anything right now?' It's so hard to enjoy feeling his breath of life when we'd prefer to die! I'm not there myself, yet, but it's my prayer for me and for you.

Heaps of love, care, affection,

Jane

A prayer

Thank you, Lord, for friends. Please help me to be a good friend to others.

The exhausted computer

Lord, I call to you for help; every morning I pray to you. Why do you reject me, Lord? Why do you turn away from me?

PSALM 88:13–14 (GNB)

A man's spirit sustains him in sickness, but a crushed spirit who can bear?

PROVERBS 18:14

There is one Lurker who can't be dealt with by stamping on his head with willpower: he just has to take his weary course. I'm talking about depression.

Everyone agrees that sadness is normal after a major loss but, to many Christians, depression is seen as failure, caused by some spiritual weakness or hidden sin. This attitude makes things extremely hard for the surprisingly large number of us who do become depressed at some time during the first five years after a 'life-crash'.

Medically recognised, reactive depression seems to descend on us when everyone (including ourselves) feels that we ought to be over the worst sadness and beginning to 'move forward again'.

However, our poor old brains are so exhausted with all the pressures, changes and constant mood-swings of the grief package that they go on strike. The chemicals in our brains cease to function properly. This plunges some into a constant state of hopeless misery and anxiety, resulting in a complete breakdown. They can't cope at work or look after themselves and need medication, rest or hospitalisation.

Others drag themselves on through life, feeling weepy, anxious, hopeless, lethargic; unable to concentrate, sleep or eat normally. They may also battle internally with a sense of being completely abandoned by God.

When I used to ask too much of my old computer, by having too many systems open at once and for too long, it would crash. It either had a complete breakdown and couldn't function at all or it switched to 'safe mode'. While flashing frequent messages pleading for specialist help, it left me with a tiny window in the centre of the screen in which to type, but it would flatly refuse to print out or let me get at my addresses or the various Bible translations and commentaries it stored. In other words, it wouldn't let me reach out to others or to God! That is exactly how I was during months of depression.

I think that many of us grind on in 'safe mode', ignoring our need for help. 'I can't go to the doctor,' some say. 'I don't want to be labelled as a nutcase, and I don't feel happy about antidepressants.' They forget that if they had pneumonia they would take the antibiotics that would save their lives. Modern antidepressants are not addictive, and, although for some people they do produce side-effects, there are so many brands on the market that doctors can usually find one that suits. I only had to take them for a short time while my system sorted itself out, but without them I might still be grinding on in a grey world of misery.

The worst part of depression for Christians is the loss of all the enjoyment we usually find in church activities, worship and private prayer. It is so easy to muddle this normal symptom of a physical illness with loss of faith. Well-meaning friends can start digging about in our spirits in their attempt to find the 'root cause' of our problem, leaving us feeling more worthless than ever.

Depression does pass, even though, at the time, we never believe that it will.

A prayer

Lord, this is the worst I ever felt! The lights have been going off, one by one, and now the last one has blown out. Total darkness! All I can hold on to is that verse which says that you, the Light of the world, shine in the darkness and the darkness has never been able to put you out (John 1:5, GNB).

The child on his shoulders

My heart is not proud, O Lord, my eyes are not haughty; I do not concern myself with great matters or things too wonderful for me. But I have stilled and quieted my soul; like a weaned child with its mother, like a weaned child is my soul within me. O Israel, put your hope in the Lord both now and for evermore.

PSALM 131

Now that we have reached the last day of our look at the Lurkers, I'd love to tell you how God used a small boy with bright red hair to speak to me during a bad 'Lurker attack'. I was standing in a crowded airport the day I set off for that tricky first holiday on my own and, at the time, I was beginning to realise I was suffering from depression.

Isn't it strange how, when you are grieving, you feel as if your outer protective layer—your skin—has been peeled off, leaving you raw, exposed and extra-sensitive? My husband had always been sure I would never find my way anywhere. (He had good grounds for his opinion!) So he always came with me or gave me detailed written instructions. While his concern made me feel loved, it also made me ridiculously dependent. So, as I clutched my hand luggage, boarding pass and passport, I felt that a panic attack was not far away.

Several planes were delayed so the airport lounge was crowded with tense travellers and bored children. To distract myself from the approaching panic, I began watching two families, each of whom had a toddler of about the same age. The first child was obviously a future rugby player. He hurled himself about among the forest of adult legs and luggage trolleys at an astonishing speed. Then, when he realised he was lost, he would scream in terror until his father came to rescue him. When the unfortunate man was completely exhausted, he firmly sat his son on his knee where the child squirmed, writhed and struggled furiously.

The other father put his toddler (the one with the bright red hair) into a backpack. As he carried him about, he pointed out interesting things until the child's head lolled forward, resting between his father's shoulders, fast asleep.

The details of the journey—which gate, which flight, which seat, how much longer, what if we are delayed overnight, all these worries that ruffled my peace—did not disturb this child at all. He trusted his father to get him where he needed to go and to provide the care he needed on the way. As I looked at that little redhead, I was reminded of a verse I have always loved.

Let the beloved of the Lord rest secure in him, for he shields him all day long, and the one the Lord loves rests between his shoulders.

DEUTERONOMY 33:12

The contrasting faces of the two fathers also struck me. One was grey with fatigue as he wrestled with his restless son; the other looked as if he was enjoying fatherhood immensely. I couldn't help wondering how God feels about fathering me!

A friend who lost her mobility, most of her sight, her marriage and her career when a brain operation went wrong wrote the following poem, which seems to set all the Lurkers nicely in place.

Large raindrops, like life's problems,
Batter our tree,
Knocking its defences aside.
Recovering later, we notice that
The source of so much wretchedness
Actually causes us to grow.

GAIL HUTSON

A prayer

Lord, I know you are willing to carry me between your shoulders like
some parents carry their babies, but I always seem to squirm and
wriggle or even run away from you—then panic when I feel lost.
Forgive me, Lord, for making fatherhood so hard for you.

Be still, and know that I am God.

PSALM 46:10

The return of spring

— Day 31 —

The agony of letting go

When Jesus saw him lying there and learned that he had been in this condition for a long time, he asked him, 'Do you want to get well?'

JOHN 5:6

Have you ever heard anyone say sadly, 'He never got over it'? How is it that some people adapt to massive losses, and even grow through them, while others disintegrate permanently? Has God broken his promise to turn their ashes into a beautiful garland? No! God is there for anyone who turns to him but he can't mend someone who isn't ready and willing.

That sounds ridiculous! Grief feels so frightful that who would want to stay trapped by it? Yet even a leading Bible character like Jacob did just that. When he was tricked into thinking his favourite son, Joseph, was dead, he 'tore his clothes, put on sackcloth and mourned for his son many days. All his sons and daughters came to comfort him, but he refused to be comforted. "No," he said, "in mourning will I go down to the grave to my son." So his father wept for him' (Genesis 37:34–35). And he probably stayed in that gloomy state until, years later, he discovered that Joseph was alive and well and living in Egypt.

Some people seem to make their tragedy a way of life; it gains the attention, love and help of other people. If their problems were solved, they would lose all that. Others stay miserable because they want the person who caused it all to feel sorry. It sounds bizarre to say it but there are people who hide in the depressing ruins of the lives they have lost because they feel safer that way. They are too terrified of the responsibilities and demands of a new life to move forward.

Another reason for continuing to live muffled in sadness is because letting go of the person you have lost is actually very difficult. Somehow you feel unfaithful to them and, by continuing to mourn their memory, you feel you can hang on to them. Letting go of a 'prodigal' child or partner can also feel like turning your back on them finally and giving up hope of their return.

When my GP said she didn't think I would come out of my depression until I let my husband go, I was furious. How could I let go of the person I'd vowed to love 'until death do us part'? Then I realised that it was not the person I needed to let go, it was the past—those 30 happy years of marriage. I was clinging tenaciously to them, willing God through intense prayer to bring my husband back to me. Then suddenly I realised that, should he come back, it would never be the same marriage again. I had changed and so had he. We would have to start again from scratch. Time can never be made to run backwards. I needed to accept the situation—just as it was—and leave it to God, whether he brought my husband home or blessed him where he was.

So I wrote a long list of all those happy memories—and the few that were not so good—and buried the document at the end of my garden under a little wooden cross. Then I turned my back on it and deliberately walked away. That was the day when I walked out of my dark prison, and gradually I began to realise that there really was a life to be enjoyed as a single woman living on my own. Even happiness was possible again, regardless of whether or not my husband returned.

A friend, facing a similar situation, wrote this poem.

Past hurt or regrets,
As difficult to leave behind
As a warm duvet,
Familiar and secure,
Comforting,
Potentially entangling,
A possible hindrance.

GAIL HUTSON

A question

'Do you want to get well?' (John 5:6).

The difference between happiness and joy

I am worn out from calling for help… Insults have broken my heart and I am in despair. I had hoped for sympathy, but there was none… I am in pain and despair; lift me up, O God… I will praise God with a song; I will proclaim his greatness by giving him thanks… The Lord listens to those in need and does not forget his people in prison.

PSALM 69:3A, 20, 29–30, 33 (GNB, ABRIDGED)

How can we ever be happy again when we've lost the person, the role or the health from which we derived our happiness? Perhaps we never will be happy again but joy is definitely possible. Happiness is linked with happenings (the two words have the same root) so, obviously, it's lost when nasty things happen to us. Joy is different. It is a quality that Jesus had, in spite of all the pressure, pain and disappointment he experienced. Joy is a supernatural emotion that bubbles away under the surface of our grief. It is not a noisy, grinning mask that we put on but a deep inner sense of well-being resulting from the sure knowledge that God is good, totally in control and there with you in the middle of the mess.

Jesus never promised us happiness in this life but he most certainly means us to have joy, which is so closely linked to peace that someone once said, 'Joy is peace dancing and peace is joy resting.'

To be honest, there were many days during my depression when the last thing I felt was joyful. Yet, even in the blackest times, little spurts of joy pierced the darkness, and I believe that these little match-flames had two main triggers.

The first is the little phrase 'I will'. King David was sometimes so full of joy that he couldn't stop himself dancing—to the great embarrassment of his wife (2 Samuel 6:14–16). Yet he was also depressed, afraid and angry. All the negative emotions are poured out freely by all the psalmists, yet a change of mood often follows the words, 'I will', as it does in verse 30 of today's psalm. The phrase 'I will…'—praise, sing, thank or proclaim God's goodness—appears in the Psalms 53 times.

I could decide to thank him, put on a praise tape or tell someone else how good he is—even though it was often the last thing I wanted to do. Yet, whenever I made myself do it, I felt that inner spark.

Perhaps joy is a mental attitude that we can cultivate with practice. I can get into bed at night and think, 'It's horrible, lying here alone' or I can say, 'Thank you, Lord, for this warm bed, the roof over my head and a nice hot-water bottle.'

Sometimes it feels obscene to thank God for the ghastly things that are happening to us. Yet we can thank him for being in the middle of them with us, and for the fact that it is his responsibility to get us through them—and out at the far end.

The other 'joy trigger' also comes from the Psalms.

Restore to me the joy of your salvation and grant me a willing spirit, to sustain me.

PSALM 51:12

That verse arrived in a card from a friend who was going through a far tougher time than I ever had, but she said:

If I argue with God about my circumstances, complain inwardly or constantly plan ways of escape—I lose my joy and my peace. If I can allow God to know what is best for me and my family and just rest in him (i.e. develop a 'willing spirit'), I find the 'joy of the Lord is my strength' (Nehemiah 8:10).

A prayer

Lord, I can't feel grateful to you for what's happened, but help me to notice all the little things you do to make the situation a tiny bit less bleak.

Whinges, 'Podding' and POMS

Do everything without complaining… so that you may become blameless and pure, children of God without fault.

PHILIPPIANS 2:14–15A (ABRIDGED)

'Do not judge, or you too will be judged. For in the same way you judge others, you will be judged.'

MATTHEW 7:1–2A

From the ends of the earth we hear singing… But I said, 'I waste away, I waste away! Woe to me!'

ISAIAH 24:16A (ABRIDGED)

There are three attitudes that we can easily slip into during grief but which smother joy like candle snuffers. They are grumbling, criticising others (I call that 'Podding'—Putting Others Down), and self-pity (the Poor Old Me Syndrome, or 'POMS').

Whinging and constant complaints were the sins that kept the people of Israel wandering aimlessly round in the wilderness for 40 years. God set them free from slavery, offered them a beautiful, fertile land of their own and provided food and water for the journey, but all they did was whinge until God became angry. He wouldn't let them into their new land until they learnt to break the habit.

Grumbling not only stifles our own joy; it also extinguishes everyone else's. It insults God, too, when we ignore all the good things he does for us by focusing all our attention on the bits of our lives (or other people) that we don't like.

When things are going wrong, we need to pour our pain into the ears of our friends. However, we do need to ration this luxury because sympathy-hunting can quickly become a habit that drives people away. Wherever you find stinging nettles, there are usually dock leaves growing nearby. They act as natural antidotes to stings. I tried hard (though often unsuccessfully) to develop the art of looking for something good in every difficult situation to act as a dock leaf.

'Podding' can also become a habit. When we have been hurt badly, trusting people can become difficult. To protect ourselves, we can build invisible walls between ourselves and others, as a defence against further pain. From the top of these thick walls, we look down on people, taking a weird sort of pleasure in spotting their faults and weakness. It also gives us a sense of power to point out our negative observations to other people, and the more we put someone else down, the better we feel about ourselves in comparison. Looking down in judgment on the world is a lonely game, cutting us off from people and from God.

POMS casts us in the role of victim or martyr, and if we do that too often we risk becoming permanently typecast. There are few things more painful than being accused of self-pity, yet an attack of the POMS can be so subtle, we don't recognise it before other people do.

This poem and quotation, sent inside a card, arrived on exactly the right day, just when I was tempted to give up completely.

'Why?'
I said,
'What did I do to deserve this?
How will I cope?
Why me?'

The Lord said,
'Don't blame me, cling to me;
Don't shut me out, call on me;
Don't question me, trust me.
I love you, I died for you;
I won't desert you now.
I see your tears.
I understand the agony in your heart.
You are not alone.
Trust me.'

ANON

The handle of my plough with tears is wet, but yet my God—keep me from turning back.

AMY CARMICHAEL

A prayer

Lord, I know that it is not what has happened to me that matters, but how I react to it. I accept responsibility for my attitudes but I do need your help with them. I could be such a glowing Christian if some of the people and problems in my life didn't exist! Help me to focus on the good things rather than the bad. And, Lord, tell me quickly whenever I begin to feel sorry for myself.

God is a gardener

The Lord will surely… make her deserts like Eden, her waste-lands like the garden of the Lord. Joy and gladness will be found in her, thanksgiving and the sound of singing.

ISAIAH 51:3 (ABRIDGED)

The desolate land will be cultivated instead of lying desolate in the sight of all who pass through it. They will say, 'This land that was laid waste has become like the garden of Eden.'

EZEKIEL 36:34–35A

The Lord will… satisfy your needs in a sun-scorched land… You will be like a well-watered garden, like a spring whose waters never fail.

ISAIAH 58:11 (ABRIDGED)

My sweetheart, my bride, is a secret garden, a walled garden, a private spring; there the plants flourish. They grow like an orchard of pomegranate trees and bear the finest fruits… I have entered my garden, my sweetheart, my bride. I am gathering my spices and myrrh.

SONG OF SONGS 4:12–13; 5:1A (GNB)

Our first garden was nothing but a building site when we returned from our honeymoon. It took years of planning, planting, weeding and clipping before we felt it was exactly how we wanted it to be. There is nothing like the pleasure of sitting in your own garden, in the cool of a summer evening, after a long day pottering in the soil. I love savouring the fragrance of the flowers and the shapes of the plants, the way the colours blend and the various textures enhance one another.

One day, we heard that the council had decided to put our village on mains drainage. At first we were glad we wouldn't have to empty the cesspit any more but then we heard that the huge drainpipes were being laid through all the back gardens in our road.

When the giant earth-movers, lorries and cranes finished their work of destruction, I stood looking at the heaps of clay, rubble and mangled plants that covered the garden we had worked on for years, and the sense of desolation was awful. Something beautiful had been desecrated and I didn't feel I had the energy to start creating another.

'I think I'll take up golf,' I sniffed.

My husband stood holding his mug of tea in silence for a long time. Then he said, 'What a wonderful chance to design a totally new garden!'

'But I don't want a new garden,' I snapped. 'I liked the old one!'

'Look at that heap of clay,' he continued, without appearing to hear. 'We could use it to make a raised patio at the end of the garden where it would catch the best sunshine. And that deep hole they dug for us would make a wonderful pond.'

A long time (and a lot of hard work) later, we had a garden that was totally different but also beautiful in its own way.

The verses at the beginning of this chapter have become so special to me since the metaphorical earth-movers devastated my life. God promises to replan and replant the ruined 'gardens' of our lives, and he pledges himself to make us beautiful again.

Jesus said, 'My Father is the gardener' (John 15:1), and

today's verses show us that he takes delight in our lives as a gardener enjoys his garden. When our 'gardens' are ruined, he takes the opportunity to create something new and even more enjoyable—so long as we let him.

But the fruit of the Spirit is love, joy, peace, patience, kindness, goodness, faithfulness, gentleness and self-control.

GALATIANS 5:22–23A

But I am like an olive tree growing in the house of God; I trust in his constant love for ever and ever. I will always thank you, God, for what you have done.

PSALM 52:8–9A (GNB)

A prayer

Jesus, you are changing me,
by your Spirit you're making me like you.
Jesus, you're transforming me,
that your loveliness may be seen in all I do.
You are the potter and I am the clay,
help me to be willing to let you have your way.
Jesus, you are changing me,
As I let you reign supreme within my heart.

MARILYN BAKER

I will change your name

You will be called by a new name, a name given by the Lord
himself. You will be like a beautiful crown for the Lord. No
longer will you be called 'Forsaken'... 'The Deserted Wife'.
Your new name will be 'God is Pleased with Her'.

ISAIAH 62:2B–4A (GNB, ABRIDGED)

Forms, forms, forms! Perhaps we all hate filling them in, but
after a life-crash they never seem to end. I remember feeling
totally traumatised when faced with the question, 'Who is
your next of kin?'

Forms also force us into facing our new and often unwelcome
identity: widow, separated, single parent, unemployed, divorced,
OAP.

'But I'm still me inside,' said a friend. 'I don't like being
put in an official category.' I remember how hard I found it to
accept my need for a wheelchair during the years when I was
ill. I did not want to be enveloped by the 'disabled person'
identity.

The word 'name' can mean identity or reputation. You can
'get a bad name' for carelessness or 'make a name for yourself'
by your success. We can also call ourselves names by thinking
of ourselves as a burden, a failure, a cripple, no use, unlovable.

Many of us also wear name-labels given to us in the past—
hidden identities that were written on our souls by parents,
teachers, aunts and siblings. They dog us into our adult lives,

even though no one else is aware of their existence. They are names like Stupid, Clumsy, Should-have-been-a-boy, Troublemaker, Ugly, Not-good-enough, In-the-way, Accident, You'll-never-make-it. Children so easily see themselves through the eyes of the adults who surround them and, once labelled, it is so hard to see ourselves any other way.

'I feel the words "victim" and "rejected" are written all over me,' said a friend who had been abused as a child and, more recently, dumped by her husband.

The verses I chose for today have become very special to me. What a promise! God is able to rub out these secret names. He wants us to start seeing ourselves as he sees us and not as other humans saw us once.

Take a minute to stop and ask God to show you, first, your inner name, and then the new one he wants to give to you. Finally, ask him to give you the faith to receive your new identity as he begins to make you into the kind of person he wants you to be.

I will change your name.
You shall no longer be called
Wounded, outcast, lonely or afraid.
I will change your name.
Your new name shall be
Confidence, joyfulness, overcoming one;
Faithfulness, friend of God,
One who seeks my face.

D.J. BUTLER

A prayer

Lord, I'm beginning to have the hope in my heart that you really can change the person I've always been—the one I've never liked. I've tried for years to change myself but I've always been aware of something 'wrong' right in the centre of myself. There is one small cog in the machine that is slightly out of line and it sets everything else off balance. Please reach right into my inner workings and fix that cog. You say in your word that 'anyone who is joined to Christ is a new being; the old is gone, the new has come' (2 Corinthians 5:17, GNB). I claim your promise because, as I come out of all these clouds of grief, I want to be different—to start all over again. Thank you for being a God of fresh starts.

To him who overcomes... I will also give him a white stone with a new name written on it, known only to him who receives it.

REVELATION 2:17

How kind he is!

Be merciful, O Lord, for I am looking up to you in constant hope. Give me happiness, O Lord, for I worship only you. O Lord, you are so good and kind, so ready to forgive; so full of mercy for all who ask your aid.

PSALM 86:3–5 (LB)

Let your favour shine again upon your servant; save me just because you are so kind!

PSALM 31:16 (LB)

Oh, put God to the test and see how kind he is! See for yourself the way his mercies shower down on all who trust in him.

PSALM 34:8 (LB)

A couple of weeks after my life-crash, I met an old friend un-expectedly in the street. He is a huge 'cuddly-bear' vicar who is so tall that his smile beamed down on me from far above my head.

'How are you all?' he asked cheerfully.

'He doesn't know… he hasn't heard the news yet,' I thought as I panicked internally.

'And how's your old man?' he continued cheerfully. I gulped and stammered out a hasty explanation and then waited for the embarrassing pause, intrusive questions, soothing platitudes or veiled condemnation that I usually encountered.

He said nothing at all. He just put two huge hands on my shoulders and, when I dared to look up, I noticed the tears pouring down his cheeks. I never saw such a look of pure compassion on anyone's face.

As I stumbled on along the busy street, feeling oddly comforted, I thought, 'How very kind he is.' He had not said or done anything—but 'kind' is something that you are before you do anything at all.

My mother loved the word 'kind'. She had a little saying, which became a recurring joke in the family—'Be kind to each other'—and if she wanted to pay someone the highest possible compliment, she would say they were 'so kind'.

Once, I was looking through the Bible she used for the last ten years of her life—the paraphrase known as the Living Bible. Throughout the Psalms, she had heavily underlined the word 'kind' every time it appears as a description of the Lord.

I love playing with words, so I looked up 'kind' in my thesaurus, and when I saw how many shades of meaning the word has, I could not help thinking that the list gives a wonderfully rich picture of the Lord's character:

Affectionate; altruistic; compassionate; congenial; considerate; courteous; friendly; generous; gentle; good; good-natured; gracious; helpful; indulgent; kind-hearted; kindly; lenient; loving; mild; obliging; philanthropic; sympathetic; tender-hearted; thoughtful; understanding.

Since the day when I met my old friend in the street, I haven't worried so much about what to say or do when I first meet someone who is going through the mill. Words and actions are not as important as what is in your heart—the kindness and compassion that flow straight from God himself. These qualities are in very short supply in our busy, self-occupied, achievement-orientated world today. When most people ask, 'How are you?' they expect the cheerful reply, 'Fine, thanks.' If you start telling them the truth, they hastily look at their watches and rush away. God has no way of showing people his kindness and compassion except through us.

Therefore, as God's chosen people, holy and dearly loved, clothe yourselves with compassion, kindness, humility, gentleness and patience.

COLOSSIANS 3:12

A prayer

Lord, surely you can't expect me to go round sloshing loving-kindness about when I'm carrying such a heavy load of grief that I'm staggering under the weight of it. How can I listen to anyone else's problems when I'm scouring the world to find someone to listen to mine? But perhaps this is your clever way of taking my mind off things. I don't have any kindness of my own left in my heart for others, so you'll just have to put some of yours in there for them!

Offering the scars

Praise be to the... Father of compassion and the God of all comfort, who comforts us in all our troubles, so that we can comfort those in any trouble with the comfort we ourselves have received from God.

2 CORINTHIANS 1:3–4 (ABRIDGED)

I felt a bit worried about sharing these kitchen verses because, on a couple of occasions, they made me so angry! I remember astounding a very well-meaning friend by bursting into tears of rage during a family tea-party at her house, back in 1982. I had only just come out of hospital after that serious viral illness had nearly cost me my life. I simply did not want to accept that it had left me with all kinds of disabilities that would probably be permanent. My six children were all still very young, and the prospect of bringing them up from a wheelchair was not pleasant.

'Never mind, Jen,' said my friend soothingly. 'Just think how you will be able to use this experience to help other people one day.' My tears did not trickle nicely down my cheeks, they came out under such pressure that their trajectory was probably horizontal. How could anything good ever come out of such a negative and destructive situation?

Actually, that friend has been proved right, although I could never have believed it at the time. Those eight years of illness enriched me (and my children) immensely and they have brought me in touch with thousands of chronically sick and disabled people all over the world.

One day, a friend rang me from Northern Ireland and said much the same about my new situation. 'God could never use a sordid mess like this!' I told her vehemently.

When our dreams are extinguished by adversity and disappointment, most of us think, 'What a pointless waste.' Yet, God does comfort us and, however much we hate the misery, there is no doubt that it has the potential to increase our compassion for others. Their grief may not have been caused by the same situation but, as I've said before, the grief itself feels much the same—and you need to have been there yourself to understand how grief feels.

About the same time as that unfortunate phone call from Northern Ireland, I found a little phrase in *Listening Prayer* by Leanne Payne: 'Lord, transform this agony into healing power for others.' That went straight up on the kitchen wall and I found myself praying it sometimes, tentatively, as I stirred a saucepan. The 'mess' did not seem quite so pointless and destructive if I could believe that God might use it creatively in some way at some time in the future. Søren Kierkegaard once wrote, 'God created everything out of nothing and everything which God is to use he first reduces to nothing.' Obviously, it's not much fun being reduced to nothing, but while it is happening it helps to know that it isn't all going to be for nothing.

A question

Have you ever considered offering your grief to God, as a special present from you to him? We may always carry the scars of our wounds but, as Jesus reaches out his hand to

127

receive our gift, we see that he is scarred too. His wounds brought us healing and he can use ours to bring comfort and hope to others who are also wounded.

A prayer

Lord, make me an instrument of thy peace.
Where there is hatred, let me sow love;
Where there is injury, pardon;
Where there is doubt, faith;
Where there is despair, hope;
Where there is darkness, light;
Where there is sadness, joy.
O Divine Master,
Grant that I may not
So much seek to be consoled as to console;
To be understood as to understand;
To be loved as to love.
For it is in giving that we receive;
It is in pardoning that we are pardoned;
And in dying that we awaken to eternal life.

FRANCIS OF ASSISI

The old apple tree

There is hope for a tree that has been cut down; it can come back to life and sprout. Even though its roots grow old, and its stump dies in the ground, with water it will sprout like a young plant.

JOB 14:7–9 (GNB)

The old apple tree was a hundred toys rolled into one. I could swing from the ropes suspended from its branches; its gnarled boughs could become a tree house, a space-rocket, a castle or simply a place to hide. In spring I could pretend to be a fairy princess enthroned in frothy pink blossom, but in the autumn the apples tasted better than anything my imagination could produce.

Then, one night in January, a fierce gale brought the old tree crashing down. Next morning I cried bitterly over the corpse laid out, bare and dead, in the soggy orchard grass.

'It'll make good firewood,' said a tactless grown-up. 'We'll leave it there to season till next winter.' The thought of my dear old tree being chopped to pieces did nothing to comfort me.

But spring came back—as it always does, even after the hardest of winters. As I was playing in the orchard one day, I was astonished to see pink blossom covering the fallen tree. The trunk had been brutally wrenched and torn by the storm but one part of it must still have been connected to root; and

I guess, during all its many years the roots of that old tree must have grown very deep indeed.

All summer the apple tree continued to be my hiding place, and in the autumn the apples tasted as good as ever. The thing that I remember most vividly about the tree is this: in the years after it blew down, only half of it produced blossom and fruit. The side that was severed from the roots soon died and eventually rotted away.

[Jesus said] 'I am the true vine, and my Father is the gardener. He cuts off every branch in me that bears no fruit, while every branch that does bear fruit he prunes so that it will be even more fruitful... Remain in me, and I will remain in you. No branch can bear fruit by itself; it must remain in the vine. Neither can you bear fruit unless you remain in me. I am the vine; you are the branches. If a man remains in me and I in him, he will bear much fruit; apart from me you can do nothing. If anyone does not remain in me, he is like a branch that is thrown away and withers; such branches are picked up, thrown into the fire and burned... This is to my Father's glory, that you bear much fruit.'

JOHN 15:1–2, 4–6, 8A

A prayer

Lord, sometimes I feel like that old tree, wrenched from its roots by a storm and left flattened, fit only for firewood. I know that my only hope of new life is to stay connected to you, so that the sap of spiritual energy can flow back into the dead carcass of all I used to be. Please show me how to remain in your love. Help me to glorify you by bearing fruit again—and dare I ask that it will taste sweeter than ever before?

The righteous will flourish like a palm tree, they will grow like a cedar of Lebanon; planted in the house of the Lord, they will flourish in the courts of our God. They will still bear fruit in old age, they will stay fresh and green.

PSALM 92:12–14

Blessed is the man who trusts in the Lord, whose confidence is in him. He will be like a tree planted by the water that sends out its roots by the stream. It does not fear when heat comes; its leaves are always green. It has no worries in a year of drought and never fails to bear fruit.

JEREMIAH 17:7–8

The mysterious finishing post

Arise from the depression and prostration in which circumstances have kept you—rise to a new life! Shine, be radiant
with the glory of the Lord, for your light has come, and the
glory of the Lord has risen upon you! ... And his glory shall
be seen on you.

ISAIAH 60:1–2 (AMP, ABRIDGED)

Acceptance is the name of the mysterious finishing post that
marks the end of the grief journey. It is not a weak resigna-
tion—a bowing down in defeat to the inevitable. Acceptance
is a strong decision of the will to use our energy to start living
again. It means saying, 'I didn't want this to happen; it was
the last thing I would have chosen; but since it has happened
I will stop hankering after all that I have lost and decide to
make the very most of what I have left.'

I think I reached that point the day I walked away from the
wooden cross at the bottom of my garden. Soon afterwards, I
was in church when the verse at the top of this page suddenly
caught my eye and I felt as if God were gently waking me, like
a child, from a long sleep.

Before I could ask him what he meant, someone at the
front was reading the story of Hannah from 1 Samuel 1. It
tells how she longed for a baby while her husband's other
wife produced them with sickening regularity—and then
mocked her for being barren. It was verse 8 that struck me:

'Her husband Elkanah would ask her, "Hannah, why are you crying? Why won't you eat? Why are you always so sad? Don't I mean more to you than ten sons?"' (GNB)

'Lord,' I scribbled down inside the cover of my Bible, 'are you asking me that question—only changing the word "sons" to "husbands"?'

Is God enough? In one way, of course, he is not. He did not design us as self-sufficient little islands; he built into our systems the need for human love and companionship (Genesis 2:18). Perhaps that is why, when we lose the person who provided all that for us, we can so easily rush into a new relationship, simply out of a sense of panic. All too often, these 'rebound relationships' are disastrous. Grief is a notorious robber of common sense.

So should we all become monks or nuns and lock ourselves up in solitary confinement? No way! But while we are demanding certain things (or people) from him, we miss his gift of contentment, which comes when we rely on him to provide what we need. It also means delighting in him for himself and not merely as a means of getting what we think we want. When he sees that we need love with skin on it, he provides a human being, and always at exactly the right time. David says, 'Delight yourself also in the Lord, and he will give you the desires and secret petitions of your heart' (Psalm 37:4, Amp).

Yes, God is enough! He can, and does, provide all we need in every possible way. The more we expect him to provide, the more he does.

You, Lord, are all I have, and you give me all I need; my future is in your hands.

PSALM 16:5 (GNB)

As we begin to emerge from the bleak, frozen winter of grief, I believe the Lord wants to say this to us.

An invitation

Come then, my love; my darling, come with me. The winter is over; the rains have stopped; in the countryside the flowers are in bloom. This is the time for singing; the song of doves is heard in the fields. Figs are beginning to ripen; the air is fragrant with blossoming vines. Come then, my love; my darling, come with me. You are like a dove that hides in the crevice of a rock. Let me see your lovely face and hear your enchanting voice.

SONG OF SONGS 2:10–14 (GNB)

The dilapidated teddy bear

The people who walked in darkness have seen a great light.
They lived in a land of shadows, but now light is shining on
them. You have given them great joy, Lord; you have made
them happy. They rejoice in what you have done... A child
is born to us! A son is given to us! And he will be our ruler.
He will be called, 'Wonderful Counsellor', 'Mighty God',
'Eternal Father', 'Prince of Peace'.

ISAIAH 9:2–3A, 6 (GNB)

Can we return, full circle, to the promise Jesus makes to all
broken people, 'to bind up the brokenhearted, to proclaim
freedom for the captives and release from darkness for the
prisoners' (Isaiah 61:1)? Not to mention his pledge to exchange our funeral ashes for a wedding garland!

You may be feeling disappointed because he seems to be
taking such a long time. I once spent weeks of work restoring
an antique teddy bear that had belonged to an elderly friend.
He needed hours of careful rejoining, darning and patching, as
well as new eyes, paws and a smart knitted suit. He spent so
long on my lap during his repair that we grew far too close to
each other ever to be parted again. It is while Jesus is mending
us that we grow close to him, too, so perhaps the longer it
takes, the better.

Thinking of that old teddy, which of your lost bits do you
need Jesus to restore? Is it your hope? Or maybe you have

mislaid your joy under the clutter of life, or your peace has been squeezed out by worry. He has the divine ability to be exactly what each one of us lacks.

Perhaps you need that tender kind of mother's love? He can rock you in his arms and soothe your fears as he sings to you (Zephaniah 3:17).

Perhaps you need a father to hold your hand in the darkness? (Isaiah 41:10).

Or that perfect husband (Isaiah 54:5), who vows to take responsibility for all your needs, both practical and emotional, and to cherish, protect and provide for you throughout life while loving you as tenderly as he loves his own body? (Ephesians 5:28).

Maybe you need his healing? I know, from personal experience, that he can mend broken bodies, but major losses damage us right through to the core of our being. The inside parts of us that think, feel, set our goals and determine our personality (as well as communicating with God)—these areas are as secret as the hidden layers of my Russian doll. Yet in Psalm 23 he promises to 'restore our souls' (v. 3).

Loneliness can feel like a horrible abyss, but Jesus promises to be the sort of friend and companion who never walks away (Hebrews 13:5). Hundreds of years ago, a woman called Julian chose to live alone in a tiny cell in Norwich, because she wanted to give all her time and attention to prayer. She tells us:

The Lord gave me a spiritual understanding of the warm friendliness of his love... He is our clothing; out of love for us he wraps us around, fastens the clasp, and enfolds us in his love, so that he will never leave us. I saw that he is everything that is good for us.

Perhaps you still feel so fragmented that you don't really know what you need Jesus to be. All that is left of you is a scattered mass of broken pieces. Remember how Jesus told his disciples, 'Gather the pieces that are left over. Let nothing be wasted' (John 6:12). The person who insisted that nothing should be lost cares intensely about the broken fragments of your life. Perhaps you simply need to ask him to come and gather you up and make you whole again.

An invitation

'Come to me, all you who labour and are heavy-laden and over-burdened, and I will cause you to rest. I will ease and relieve and refresh your souls.'

MATTHEW 11:28 (AMP)

Conclusion

It must have been about four years after my husband left that I was walking down the lane near my home one afternoon in early spring. As I was admiring a clump of snowdrops on a mossy bank, I suddenly felt an old, almost forgotten sensation spreading all over me. It was happiness—not the poignant, intense spurts of supernatural joy that had kept me going through the gloom of the previous years, but real, ordinary, down-to-earth happiness.

It does return, however hard it sometimes is to believe that it ever will. As we recover from loss, that heavy, sad feeling can actually become a permanent part of us, unless we deliberately decide to throw it off. When happiness takes us by surprise one day, as we plant some seeds, bake a cake or watch a sunset, we sometimes recoil, almost guiltily. Are we afraid to enjoy something without the person we have lost, because we feel we will lose them for ever if we begin to enjoy a new-shaped life? Or maybe we cannot bear the thought of not being able to share the enjoyment with them? Sometimes, if we are still blaming ourselves for what happened, we feel we don't deserve to be happy again. Whatever the reason for our reluctance, we hastily dismiss the disturbing new emotion and return to plodding on in our heavy black garb of sorrow.

Yet happiness should be welcomed, embraced and given permission to stay. We cannot keep our lost people with us by mourning them for ever and, if they were worth loving in the first place, the one thing they would want for us is our happiness. So we must grant ourselves the right to be happy without them and also to enjoy life as it is, however new or limited it may feel.

For me, snowdrops have always marked the start of spring. They are the tiny, pale pointers to the glorious profusion of colour that will fill the flower beds in a few months' time. After that walk down the lane, I began to hunt for 'snowdrops' in my life. I mean the small things that I was beginning to like about living alone: the freedom to have the light on and read at night without keeping someone else awake, or eating what I fancied on a tray by the TV and without watching football! Happiness is not so much an emotion as an act of the will, a choice we can make, regardless of the outer circumstances of our lives. I believe we can achieve this by deciding to stop ruminating constantly on all the lovely things we have lost and deliberately beginning to hunt each day for 'snowdrops'—the little things that are beginning to make life feel worth living again.

Do not cling to events of the past or dwell on what happened long ago. Watch for the new thing I am going to do. It is happening already—you can see it now!

ISAIAH 43:18–19A (GNB)

One of my favourite kitchen verses says, 'Who is this coming up from the desert leaning on her lover?' (Song of Songs 8:5). Someone saw it there once and said, 'Yes, the Lord certainly loves a good leaner!' Learning to lean is definitely what my journey of adjustment has been all about. You do experience genuine peace when you suddenly realise that you have survived the event that has always been your worst fear—not only survived it but actually seen how God was able to turn the whole situation round to bring you good (Romans 8:28). This realisation breaks the power of fear. You know for sure that whatever may happen in the future, God will carry you through it, as he has carried you this time—just so long as you are willing to be a good leaner! When you know from personal experience just how able he is to hold you up, then you really do know peace.

Two final prayers

Fill us each morning with your constant love, so that we may sing and be glad all our life. Give us now as much happiness as the sadness you gave us during all our years of misery.

PSALM 90:14–15 (GNB)

Take all my broken purposes and disappointed hopes and use them to make thy perfect rainbow arch. Take all my clouds of sadness and calamity and from them make thy sunset glories. Take my night and make it bright with stars. Take my ill-health and pain until they accomplish in thy purpose as much as health could achieve. Take me as I am with impulses, strivings, longings so often frustrated and thwarted, and even with what is broken and imperfect make thy dreams come true. Through him, who made of human life a sacrament, of thorns a crown, of a cross a throne, even through Jesus Christ my Lord. Amen.

DR LESLIE WEATHERHEAD, *A PRIVATE HOUSE OF PRAYER*

Bereavement

Bible readings for special times

Jean Watson

This book of 24 undated reflections draws comfort and inspiration from the Bible and from experience for those who are going through a time of bereavement, as well as providing insight for those wanting to support others who are bereaved. Jean Watson suggests how it might feel to get through the dark days and to move, however slowly, from 'getting by' with help, to 'getting a life' in which living with loss goes alongside the gains in terms of new insights on faith and life and a greater ability to empathise with others.

ISBN 978 0 85746 326 5   £3.99
Available from your local Christian bookshop or direct from BRF: please visit www.brfonline.org.uk.

Also from BRF

I'm fine!

Removing masks and growing into wholeness

Wendy Billington

In this book Wendy Billington gently explores ways of helping people remove the 'I'm fine!' mask and grow through the challenges posed by issues such as loneliness, low self-esteem and parenting pain, as well as a variety of addictive behaviours. Those struggling with particular problems in their lives may feel they can't be honest about their circumstances even— perhaps especially—in a church context. Isolation, shame, and anxiety about how others will perceive them can add to their difficulties, compounding them with a sense of being locked in with the problem.

Using case studies, Bible teaching and practical guidelines, Wendy shows how church members can support one another, not only helping individuals but building a community that is characterised by loving, sensitive pastoral care.

ISBN 978 184101 871 3   £7.99
Available from your local Christian bookshop or direct from BRF: please visit www.brfonline.org.uk.

Also available for Kindle: see www.brfonline.org.uk/ebooks.

Enjoyed

this book?

Write a review—we'd love to hear what you think.
Email: reviews@brf.org.uk

Keep up to date—receive details of our new books as they happen.
Sign up for email news and select your interest groups at:
www.brfonline.org.uk/findoutmore/

Follow us on Twitter @brfonline

By post—to receive new title information by post (UK only), complete
the form below and post to: BRF Mailing Lists, 15 The Chambers, Vineyard,
Abingdon, Oxfordshire, OX14 3FE

Your Details
Name _____
Address_____
_____
Town/City _____ Post Code _____
Email_____

Your Interest Groups (*Please tick as appropriate)	
☐ Advent/Lent	☐ Messy Church
☐ Bible Reading & Study	☐ Pastoral
☐ Children's Books	☐ Prayer & Spirituality
☐ Discipleship	☐ Resources for Children's Church
☐ Leadership	☐ Resources for Schools

Support your local bookshop
Ask about their new title information schemes.